Transforming Corporate Culture

---

9 Natural Truths
for Being Fit to Compete

Lisa Jackson
Gerry Schmidt, PhD

TRANSFORMING CORPORATE CULTURE
9 Natural Truths for Being Fit to Compete

ISBN: 978-0-9846485-0-4 (pbk)
Library of Congress Control Number: 2011909818

Printed in the United States of America

Cover design and interior layout by Rosamond Grupp
Illustration by David Boatwright
Copy Editor: Sherry Law

Requests for permission to make copies of
any part of this book can be made to:
www.CorporateCulturePros.com

10 9 8 7 6 5 4 3 2 1

To Ian, Dargan, Emily and Tyler.

And

*To all leaders who seek greatness through others.
The selfless service we perform is to make your world better.*

We also want to acknowledge a few great thinkers on change and culture, whose influence has been tremendous in shaping our work and approach: John Kotter, Jim Collins, Daniel Pink, Ram Charan, Lou Gerstner, Jack Welch, Malcolm Gladwell, Jeanne Liedtka, Robert Rosen and Robert Wiltbank.

And finally, many thanks to the numerous friends and colleagues who helped us make this book better, including David Boatwright, Doug Jenkins, David Snyder, Lee Roche, Sherry Law, Pam Prisk, as well as the many clients whose stories were told to illustrate important lessons about change in business.

Defining Change

The concept of change is very broad and conveys different meanings depending on how it's used. Here we offer the context for change that guided the writing of this book.

Random House lists 33 definitions for the word "change." (Another indication of the vast importance and challenges inherent in this concept). A few are relevant to this book:

Change – verb, noun, verb (used with object).

1. to make the form, nature, content, future course, etc., of (something) different from what it is or from what it would be if left alone: *to change one's name; to change one's opinion; to change the course of history.*

2. to transform or convert (usually fol. by *into*): *The witch changed the prince into a toad.*

3. to become different: *Overnight the nation's mood changed.*

4. to pass gradually into (usually fol. by *to* or *into*): *Summer changed to autumn.*

How are we using the word "change"?

We use change to connote BOTH forces on the outside that create pressure and demand for something new and different, AND your response to those forces. Terms like "adapt, transform, and evolve" indicate your response. In this book we focus on the intersection of external pressure AND internal response.

The best, most adaptive cultures don't happen through architecting massive changes in strategy or execution, but rather they happen when leaders inspire their teams to make small changes in their approach to planning, decision making, teamwork, and collaboration.

Transforming Corporate Culture reflects a simple and profound meaning that is relevant to business leaders: If you look at how nature works, you will see that change happens naturally and without resistance, fanfare, and sometimes without notice.

We believe business can benefit from seeking to parallel the way nature leads change. We chose 9 lessons from nature, and organized this book around them. Together, they will help leaders build more adaptive workplace cultures that are friendly to change and which create shared ownership for making the business grow and thrive.

Most of all, the term change is intended to connote the mantra we use in our work with clients:

"Organizations don't change. People do."

95% of the population are not "natural-born change agents" - it takes conscious effort, a strong motive, and a lot of practice to become comfortable stepping outside your comfort zone – and leading others to do the same.

A leader's job is to go first.

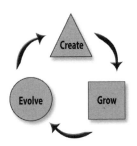

Contents

Why We Wrote This Book

When I (Lisa) was growing up, my parents kept a vase in their bedroom that reminded me of Aladdin's lamp: A large, round bottom with a narrow neck. The vase was about three feet tall, and made from the thick green glass that was common in old-style telephone pole insulators. I used to wish that if I rubbed it, magic would come out.

Every night, my parents would drop their spare change into that vase. I would often watch that ritual and think, "That's not much money. Just 10 cents. What is the point of dropping 10 cents in there?" There were a LOT of pennies (an amount so insignificant, most people wouldn't stop to pick one up). I was always excited when they threw a dollar bill into the vase. That seemed like REAL money.

I don't think there was much forethought to the ultimate outcome of this little habit – at least not initially. But the vase was easy to put money into and not easy to take money out of, so the money stayed. They didn't use it for parking meters or the pizza delivery guy, even in years when resources were lean. I think it took about five years before the money covered the entire bubble-bottom of the vase and reached the neck.

When I turned 18, that vase funded a great holiday for our family. From a small inspiration came a grand road trip of interesting experiences and time together, during which we made the decision to move to Colorado. Through that simple daily practice, formed a habit. Over time, that habit led to a major change in the lives of three people.

Cultures transform through a deposit of very specific and consistent actions, over time these deposits are like compound interest: They exponentially foster an environment in which the business can thrive and grow.

Since change is the one sure thing about life on the planet, it is nice to think that we could live in alignment with it. To remember that *everything* operates within a dynamic process of constant change: life and death, day and night, up and down, cause and effect. "Change is the new steady state," a client said to us recently.

But most of us don't feel we can have a big impact – instead feeling we are somewhat at the mercy of the larger systems we are a part of. The daily focus for most leaders reading this book – might I daresay the daily *struggle* – is how to gracefully and effectively align ourselves with the dynamic, unexpected, unpredictable roller coaster of change and remain centered and steady. This is true whether your goal is to:

- Expand insight, thought and conversation about leadership.
- Make your work and job enjoyable again.
- Win the hearts and minds of those whom you hope to influence.
- Leave a better world for the next generation.
- Create simpler ways to attend to the complexities of working in teams and organizations.

Leaders, seize the opportunity and challenge yourselves!

How Do You Change a Culture?

Having been involved in numerous large-scale culture change projects over the past 15 years, we have seen them from the vantage points of both success and failure. When change didn't work, we have usually found that it was conceived in too large a box and not connected to a shared purpose or meaning that ignites people's imagination. And too often, culture change is a mysterious phrase to describe the "broken personality" of an organization, implying its problems stem from misguided leaders who don't "get it" and employees who aren't accountable. When the conversation surrounding culture is divisive or adversarial – or it is viewed as a complicated process or a painful excuse for why a company or team is not succeeding – this does not support real change.

Reframing the Culture Conversation

We want to help people understand that culture is an essential driver of success in a knowledge economy and that changing a culture is much simpler than you think. Preserving the essential DNA of what makes you great *and* making small changes to be more adaptive – that is the leadership we need in organizations today. This view of culture is friendlier, more hopeful, and more actionable. As one of our clients said recently, "If you have kids, at some point you realize they come in the way they are, and your job as a parent is to help them be the *best* they can be with who they already *are*." Changing culture is often as simple as one leader answering the question, "What can I do to help you succeed in your job, own your part, commit to achievable goals, and enjoy your work?"

There is urgency for us in creating this conversation. Many of our friends, colleagues and clients are deeply concerned about a lack of leadership in our world, at a time where it is more needed than ever. Many leaders we know are asking, "How do we change our culture?" and finding the answers too overwhelming or complex.

We wrote this book as our coins in the vase. We hope that by offering what we have learned during 72 years (between the two of us) observing people and leading change, a few people around the world will dig deeper into their own pockets for their small change, and add it to the vase.

Enjoy this deposit of *Small Change* into your life.

Best wishes to you in finding *your* vase.

Introduction

*"Here, you see, it takes all the running
you can do to keep in the same place. If
you want to get somewhere else, you must
run at least twice as fast as that!"*

— **The Red Queen to Alice in** *Through the Looking Glass*

Wednesday, 6:00 P.M. The meeting was over and everyone felt the desire to celebrate. Nothing substantive had changed yet. In the background, an almost undetectable, palpable feeling of possibility hangs in the air: "What could happen if…?" "Remember when we…?"

We had just left a crucial meeting with leaders inside an iconic technology company discussing their future.

For four years, they had been attempting to make a strategic shift to more effectively compete in the growth market in their industry. For four years, they had failed to make the fundamental changes necessary to do so. This discussion about the future was not a "nice to have" initiative. This was about securing the company's future. Their very life depends on getting it right. The client (let's call him Dan) said it well: "This is like extreme skiing – once you go off the cliff, you have to land on your feet or you die. We have to get this right, or all of our jobs and the future of our company are truly at risk."

Through a series of 23 in-depth interviews with individuals at this company, we listened to the same story we have seen unfold in dozens of companies over the past several years:

- "Our culture is not friendly to change."

- "We make excuses all over the place for why our products don't have what customers want. Our competitors are not making those excuses."

- "We have no idea what our vision is….We just keep saying the right words and cutting resources."

- "We have the technical know-how to make this happen. We don't have the will-power."

- "We can't keep going in this direction and be here in 10 years: We'll be a sadder, smaller _____ by then." (This one tugged at our heartstrings – this company go away? A sad day for America.)

There were a lot of *extremely* skeptical people surrounding the latest efforts to make this new strategy work. Too many false starts had buried their energy and hope in a winter-like ground freeze. At the same time, we watch the human spirit in its finest state: A few new leaders, some fresh energy, and once again hope had poked its head out like a spring crocus, "Maybe this time it could actually work."

6:30 PM. After the last round of checking e-mail, about 12 of us decided to gather at a restaurant for a little wine, dinner and camaraderie (even though no budgets were allowed for such celebrations and hadn't been for several years). I sat next to one of the leaders (we'll call him Bill). Bill was charged with making the technology work – no small feat. The company was betting its future on its ability to develop world-class software. But like a field that has been planted for two decades with no tilling or soil replenishment, their software code base was archaic. Amid a multi-billion dollar revenue decline, they were facing life-or-death investment choices to upgrade their software platform and development processes. But the necessary decisions were not all within Bill's scope. Nor was it clear who *should* be making them (people up or across the line?) – or in some cases, what those decisions even were.

Yet, behind this lurking crisis the conversations were lively – lots of healthy, honest dialogue about the future dancing amongst everyone. A match had lit the fire: There was energy; there was possibility. As I listened to Bill talk about his vision and ideas, he described his relationship with the relatively new CEO of the company (to whom he does not directly report).

I turn to him at one point and asked, "What is _____'s (CEO) vision for your organization's future, amid so much change?"

Bill's response: "I don't know. We haven't heard about that."

The Perfect Storm and the Power of Culture

We sat with that conversation for weeks, pondering its irory and significance.

Here is a legacy technology company under huge pressure to compete faster and better – and knows it – but is failing to adapt. Their ability to definitively win in their industry's growth market is at risk. Their story is increasingly common: Between 2000-2010, they fell more than 60 places on the Fortune 500, out of their Top 100 slot (even with a significant strategic acquisition). Savvy tech companies like Amazon, HP, and Apple rocketed past them. Their revenues decreased 21% but more importantly, profits fell a stunning 57%. Here's the real kicker: This company was featured in the media and leadership books as an example of an effective turnaround – while in decline! Equally disturbing, key leaders inside the company cannot simply describe the CEO's vision (the most important predictor of speed and focus in any organization). People in the trenches of this company are desperate for a vision of *meaningful* change to recapture their stardom, and growing increasingly cynical from a constant diet of reorganization and budget cuts and cries to "do more with less!" In a time where a top concern of CEOs and boards is the shortage of sufficient leadership talent to grow, this organization has no formal talent management process or leadership development program, and has invested well below competitors in developing its leaders. The senior executive ranks are focused on "making the numbers" and have no inspiring vision beyond that. This is no criticism intended for the difficult job of today's CEOs; a similar story is playing out in numerous companies today.

This situation reflects the conditions of a society in a perfect storm: A swirling era of challenging conditions brought on by Internet transparency, globalization, and shifting demographics. In nature, growth and death are normal and natural –an entity either adapts or goes extinct. In an age of increased competition, no business is protected from the storm forces of increased competition for talent, customers. Leaders in companies of every size and in every industry are being called to re-examine Darwin's credo: To survive and be fit, you *have* to compete better. You have to take a stand and make hard choices about your market and brand, even while you face greater uncertainty about your future. You must innovate better, execute faster, and grow while becoming leaner.

Culture is at the eye of this hurricane: The calm, powerful, centered ability of your organization to win the Darwin game. Culture is what allows you to be in enough alignment to adapt quickly, build sustained growth, and compete in a global economy (even when you're local).

Why Culture?

Our opening story illustrates a growing truth and concern in our work: Far too many workplaces are not only ill-prepared to truly compete in a global, flat world – but they aren't much fun to work for either! People are burned out, suffering from change-fatigue, and tired of assuming greater workloads due to endless leaning efforts. People today are seeking *more*. We all want to do business with companies who *give* more, to work for leaders who *care* more, to create a life that *means* more. Yes, winning is the game of business. But culture is the condition of your team and playing field – and every coach knows how important these elements are to winning. Culture underpins your ability to become *fit to compete* AND to re-engage managers and employees who are frustrated, fearful of change, and fed up with constant diet of "do more with less."

Corporate cultures are weak in today's society – and they are growing weaker. Whether you're a small family business or a large legacy Fortune 100, culture is the answer to sustainable growth. If you want to win, you must accept that culture really *does* matter.

Culture is also just a fancy word for a set of deliberate practices that build alignment and friendliness toward growth and change: The single most important ingredient in your ability to detect opportunity and move faster. Culture is also your legacy and responsibility as a leader. Creating a great place to work pays big dividends (research proves it) – and dividends are what any smart investor is looking for.

These lessons from nature can help a leader more effectively tap an organization's cultural infrastructure to become more friendly toward necessary change. Unfortunately, the majority of today's workplaces are anything *but* this. They're stressed, overloaded, burned out, and *fed up*.

Evidence of a Transformational Era

What does an era of transformation look like?

My great aunt, who was born in Illinois in 1896 and lived to be 105 years old, knew people who had crossed the prairie in a covered wagon and had seen astronauts walk on the moon.

Fast forward and accelerate another century and anything imagined in the 1960's Jetson's cartoon will surely be far surpassed!

A few interesting facts to highlight transformation at work – and the need for our leaders to respond:

Economy & Business

In 2007, the World Economic Forum dropped America from first to seventh place in its ranking of nations' preparedness to benefit from advances in information technology.

Foreigners finance approximately two-thirds of U.S. domestic investment, compared with about one-fifteenth a decade ago.

In a recent study of over 100 companies, 70% said they are experiencing "moderate to major leadership shortages; 82% say they expect it to get worse; and 63% say it is starting to impact their business growth and decision making – but less than 1/3 follow leadership development best practices, or even have a talent management program.[6]

Jobs

Gallup has tracked the engagement levels of the U.S. working population for the past decade. Its most recent employee engagement research shows that 28% of American workers are engaged; 54% are not engaged; and 18% are actively disengaged.

Nearly 60% of the patents filed with the United States Patent and Trademark Office in the field of information technology now originate in Asia.

Eight engineers can be hired in India for the cost of one in the United States. Five chemists can be employed in China for the cost of one in the United States.[7]

Health

Lousy bosses can kill you – literally. A 2009 Swedish study tracking 3,122 men for ten years found that those with bad bosses suffered 20 to 40 percent more heart attacks than those with good bosses. Many studies show that for more than 75 percent of employees, dealing with their immediate boss is the most stressful part of the job.

Americans are increasingly obtaining health care overseas, where (according to The Washington Post) dentists "charge one-fifth to one-fourth of U.S. prices."

In 2001, a patient in Strasbourg, France, had his gallbladder removed by a surgeon in New York who was using a remotely controlled robot. (We hope there was a backup surgeon in the room!)

In the U.S., healthcare costs are projected to become 20% of the national economy by 2020. One-third of U.S. adults are obese, and health spending on this group grew 80% from 2001 to 2006, to $166.7 billion. Experts say 70% of those costs could be prevented through lifestyle modification – an opportunity for change if there ever were one!

Science and Technology

American companies spend three times more on litigation than on research.

In 2000, the United States was in first place for broadband Internet access; now it ranks 16th. South Korea has nearly twice the subscribers per capita of the United States.

The United States is a net importer of high-technology products. In fact, Americans now pay almost as much to foreign firms for imports as they pay to their own government in taxes.

iPod was a game-changer but who would have thought it would make Apple the #1 music company (as of June 2010)? We predict within 5 years (Hello iPad!), Apple will be the world's #1 or #2 publishing company.[8]

Political

A city in Pennsylvania not long ago considered adopting the slogan "Pittsburgh can become the Bangalore of America."

In just 7 years the United States has tripled its foreign debt. The United States' bargaining power at the global table is weakening.

Gallup and Blessing White[1] have both done extensive research on "employee engagement" and its impact on business performance. Engaged employees care about the future of the company and are willing to invest extra discretionary effort. Disengaged employees don't. Out of 17 million employees surveyed (statistics are from 2010), less than one-third (28-29%) say they are actively engaged at work. More distressing is that 54% of employees report they are *not* engaged: They float through each workday "doing time" with no passion. And about 17% report being *actively* disengaged – disgruntled people who are hard to work with, sabotage others' efforts, and stir up workplace conflict. Gallup estimates this situation costs organizations $300 billion in lost productivity every year. It is deeply concerning that in affluent societies where basic necessities are more than met, people are spending 2/3 of their life energy in situations that *fail* to tap the one thing everyone cares about: Building something meaningful together.

If you don't believe the majority of people are burned out and fed up at work, ask 10 people around you "Do you love your job? Do you love your company?" Listen to their answers. There's your evidence.

Further, attempts to adapt are not working well either: Research shows that 70-75% of all change initiatives FAIL[2] – whether an acquisition, reorganization, technology implementation, or any new direction or idea to improve the business. (No study we found quoted better than a 60% success rate for change efforts – including project management.) Either initiatives do not produce the expected growth or gain, or they simply don't work (i.e., the change never takes hold and is abandoned).

Can you name any other activity in any organization in which failure was so high, in which leaders wouldn't seriously question the risk and find ways to mitigate it? A whole industry has emerged – change management – to try. Even so, decisions are still being made every day inside companies of every size to initiate risky changes that will not and cannot work – usually because the culture cannot support them. Even with sophisticated models and approaches, failure is still more likely than success; and there is little understanding or appreciation for what it really takes to succeed. As a result, many promising growth initiatives have a *negative* impact on leaders' efforts to build positive morale, execute their mission, and secure financial performance.

For these reasons (massive workforce disengagement, high failure rates of change efforts AND the accelerating pace of change), becoming adaptive is a *crucial capability* for every leader and organization today. And, since only about 5% of people are truly "natural born change agents" and the known failure rate of businesses is about 40% in 10 years - it is *urgent* to train and develop leaders who can lead change … or find yourself at the mercy of bigger, better competitors who have figured it out.

Eat on YOUR terms. Or BE eaten. Take your pick.

Table 1. Changing Expectations in Global Work Environments

In The Face of Change Employees Want …	In The Face of Change, Leaders …
More information about: "Where are we going?" and "What does success look like?"	Are unclear why people don't commit and understand the priorities – when everyone was told (once, in an email).
Clarity about changing/conflicting priorities and objectives, but often lack the skill to effectively prioritize, especially in today's rapid-change environments.	With 100% (+) responsibility for goals and meeting the numbers, often don't effectively transfer responsibility and hand-offs to others
To avoid feeling "in the dark."	Are over committed and frustrated about how to build commitment and get others to own the results.

The good news: Success leaves a trail. Like tracking in the woods, the markers may be in plain sight but not easy to spot for the untrained hiker. The best method for leading in a dynamic, uncertain time is to build a workplace culture that focuses on turning failure rates into stories of success.

This book was written to show you how – and boil it down to small, simple practices and ideas used by successful change leaders who have done it.

Myths of Culture

During the past 15 years, we have coached and trained hundreds of leaders seeking to align their organization's culture with their efforts to grow and change.

We have been surprised by how consistently executives – regardless of organization size or industry – have struggled to understand and work with basic rules of effective organizational culture and change. Big rollouts, campaigns, and change management programs often fail because they are too event-driven and don't integrate – and steadily embed adaptability – into people's existing work-flow.

Based on hundreds of conversations we have had with leaders who are attempting to drive meaningful change in their organizations, there are three common myths we address related to change and culture:

Myth #1: Culture change is necessary – but it's long-term, difficult, and expensive.

Truth: Culture is not separate from you as the leader. (Proof: Where does your culture go at night when nobody is in the building?) Culture is how people work together that either helps or hinders achievement of vision and strategies. Creating an adaptive culture is like building a healthy body: There is no magic pill or universal approach that works for everyone. Adopting change-friendly habits in planning, communicating, teamwork, decision making, and rewards/incentives teaches people to embrace change. This works best when leaders embed habits that blend with the existing DNA, versus attacking it. (That being said there are some companies and industries that need new DNA.) Leading a large-scale culture change across a company is not for the faint of heart. But leading an effort to make your culture faster, more adaptive and better able to compete is simple and anyone can do it.

Myth #2 – People fear and resist change.

Truth: People do not resist change. People resist *being* changed. The constant suspense and pawn-moving that goes on in most organizations today leaves little stable ground to stand on. The problem with most change initiatives is not the people – it's the process. Leaders rarely initiate change in a way that makes sense to people, or make it digestible. This is why people resist, drag their feet, and engage in turf battles. As a result of the recent business climate (and companies who pursued financial success at the expense of their employees and customers), people have a low tolerance for manipulation and a high BS meter. Leaders are rarely connected and engaged enough with customers and employees (and too often "architect" changes for months behind closed doors). When you lead an intelligent process focus on telling the truth, make people part of the solution, and consciously provide a way to grow and learn, you see anticipation, exhilaration, relief (someone is *leading!*), and excitement about the future.

Myth #3 – Our culture must change so we can "do more with less."

Truth: If there is one modern-day leadership trap of our times, it's the belief "we can do it all." You *may* be able to do it all (depending on how you define "all"), but not all at once. Change succeeds by narrowing your focus, your timeline, and your target. Change fails when leaders keep starting things and stop nothing. Lisa has a rule in her household: Every time she brings home something new (clothing, household item, furniture), an equivalent number of items must leave the house – thrown away, donated, sold. Less really IS more – so please flip the equation and think about doing more *better*, not just more! (we are talking about projects not people – we do *not* mean when you hire someone, you fire someone!).

If you want your company to be competitive, innovative, and sale-able, bust these outdated myths. In a global, flat economy, culture is the true north that will help get all hands on deck to ensure you sail out of the storm.

Leading a large-scale culture change across a company is not for the faint of heart. But leading an effort to make your culture faster, more adaptive and better able to compete is simple and anyone can do it.

The Storm Forces

To understand the broader context of what is happening in our world today – and where we're headed - it's helpful to understand where we have come from. Thus, a brief exploration of the history of major change in our human community.

In her book *"Navigating the Badlands,"*[3] futurist and strategist Mary O'Hara Devereaux lays out a historical perspective based on eight disruptive innovation cycles dating to 3500 B.C. In 2005, after numerous discussions with clients saying, "We can no longer make sense of what's happening around us," she put a research team together composed of economists, sociologists, political scientists, anthropologists, strategists, and business leaders. They performed extensive research on transformations of societies during these cycles, revealing insights into the patterns of how major periods of innovation affect society.

"Every few hundred years in Western history there occurs a sharp transformation. Within a few short decades, society rearranges itself – its worldview; its basic values; its social and political structure; its arts; its key institutions. Fifty years later, there is a new world. And the people born then cannot even imagine the world in which their grandparents lived and into which their own parents were born. We are currently living through just such a transformation."

— Peter Drucker, 1993

According to Devereaux's research, the average time period of a major innovation cycle is about 75 years. The Information Revolution is a profound disruptive innovation cycle; she refers to this time in history as the greatest upset since the dawn of writing (3,500 years ago when the Sumerians of ancient Mesopotamia began written documentation on clay tablets). Currently, we are about 55 years into it.

From the vantage point of over 5,000 years and eight well-defined cycles, Devereaux shows that during major transformational eras, the old systems crumble and totally new systems, models, and ways of interacting emerge to replace them: new systems of political governance; new systems of economy, marketplace and commerce; new systems of education and resource management. If history repeats itself, the children born in 2050 will not recognize the world we experience today. This evolution is a natural progression, and from it will emerge great innovation and progress.

But in the midst of it, there are growing pains and discomfort. From the perspective of the past decade (2000-2010), we can see those happening within the corporate and government systems in our own country.

In *"Leaders at all Levels,"* **4** thought-leader Ram Charan says we are currently in a "crisis of leadership." He highlights the lack of development of true leaders who can manage increasingly diverse styles of people, situations, and opportunities – regardless of title or level.

Leadership development, talent management and succession planning endeavors are sprouting up everywhere - evidence of the growing agreement in our society's corporations that we need to develop true leaders.

But we do not believe the central issue at stake will be addressed simply by creating programs to develop more leaders. With the stakes higher than ever, we must address this question: "Are we allowing true leaders to emerge and take responsibility for driving massive change in an era of transformation across our global society?" It's not easy to lead change. It requires a great reservoir of courage and commitment to adapt and change the way people work together, the way we govern, and the way we create value in our society - especially when such leadership means a major disruption of a system that measures success and value by one yardstick: Quarterly profit and growth.

We need a growing power base of leaders to courageously address essential questions with new solutions:

- **How do we manage stability amidst efforts to reinvent economics, government, and corporate power?**

- **How do we prepare the next generation to lead in conditions that are mostly unknown?**

- **In a global society (or company) how do we create unified purpose and local empowerment?**

- **How do we build better products with less cost and waste?**

- **How do we better connect people inside companies with the needs of their customers?**

Leading in a Permanent Crisis

"The danger in the current economic situation is that people in positions of authority will hunker down. They will try to solve the problem with short-term fixes: tightened controls, across-the-board cuts, restructuring plans. They'll default to what they know how to do in order to reduce frustration and quell their own and others' fears. Their primary mode will be drawing on familiar expertise to help their organizations weather the storm.

"That risk increases if we draw the wrong conclusions from our likely recovery from the current economic downturn. Many people survive heart attacks, but most cardiac surgery patients soon resume their old ways: Only about 20% give up smoking, change their diet, or get more exercise. In fact, by reducing the sense of urgency, the very success of the initial treatment creates the illusion of a return to normalcy. The medical experts' technical prowess, which solves the immediate problem of survival, inadvertently lets patients off the hook for changing their lives to thrive in the long term. High stakes and uncertainty remain, but the diminished sense of urgency keeps most patients from focusing on the need for adaptation.

"People who practice what we call *adaptive leadership* do not make this mistake. Instead of hunkering down, they seize the opportunity of moments like the current one to hit the organization's reset button. They use the turbulence of the present to build on and bring closure to the past. In the process, they change key rules of the game, reshape parts of the organization, and redefine the work people do."[5]

Leading Transformation and Change: A Role Model

It is not the strongest of the species that survives, nor the most intelligent, but the one most responsive to change.

— **Charles Darwin**

To provide a role model for the leadership needed to truly transform and change the way we work, we turn to the top expert at change: Nature herself.

Experts estimate there are between 5 and 100 million species of plants and animals on earth. Only about two million species are known (The National Science Foundation's "Tree of Life" project).

Each of these life forms has a different purpose and set of requirements for sustaining itself. In the thick of all this complexity, life goes on without a great deal of complaint or resistance. Overall, the natural world works in pretty good harmony and order.

Contrast this complex, chaotic situation – which somehow works perfectly – with the fundamental paradigm on which we have built our societies (and organizations) for 200 years: the universe as a machine (which emerged from the Industrial Age). A machine paradigm says "If I do X, Y will predictably happen." If a part is broken, it can be fixed and the whole system will work again. If I take the system apart, I can understand the whole system by analyzing each part. We have attempted to map a machine paradigm onto managing people; separated "thinking" from "doing" in organizations; created an addiction to productivity; and broken organizations into disconnected pieces. This paradigm still dominates how modern-day business is conducted. But as the storms of change gather intensity, this paradigm is cracking under the pressure.

If you study nature and how it evolves – particularly in fast-growth, chaotic environments with extreme conditions – you gain powerful insight into how today's leaders can structure and run their teams and companies more efficiently and effectively. Through the paradigm of nature, we see that adapting happens best through small, manageable changes made gradually – with occasional sweeping big "shots" of change (e.g., tsunamis and hurricanes). Biological science and the history of evolution offer great lessons that we can apply to a revolution of leadership.

In the decades we have been working with leaders and companies (many in great trouble), we have seen the power of migrating toward leadership based on the natural and biological world. This migration requires openness to mindsets and attitudes that most leaders are not trained in. But courageous and committed leaders who want to learn will find they achieve their strategies and goals more effortlessly.

These are the leaders who say, "Change begins with ME." And *mean* it.

All great innovations in our world have been born from such a choice.

A Final Word ... Before We Begin

"People travel to wonder at the height of the mountains, at the huge waves of the seas, at the long course of the rivers, at the vast compass of the ocean, at the circular motion of the stars, and yet they pass by themselves without wondering."

— St. Augustine

Volumes have been written about leadership and culture – what it is, how you identify and cultivate it in people, and what's required to make it a systematic, measurable driver of your business.

We did not set out to invent a new formula for leadership and change here. There are already several approaches, many of which are not working well (often built on outdated paradigms about learning, control, and hierarchy). Second, *every leader is different. You* have to find what works for *you*: What works for one person won't work for someone else in a different set of circumstances.

In writing this book, we thoughtfully considered two questions based on seven combined decades of observing and modeling leaders:

1) "What do the leaders we knew – who have succeeded in leading change – *do* that is replicable?"

2) "What are the fundamental mindsets that lead to an ability – and responsibility – inside a person to *lead others* on a successful journey of change?"

Our purpose in this book is to offer a menu of shortcuts and practices to embed change-friendly culture behaviors within yourself, your team and your organization. We chose to highlight the characteristics of successful change that *leaders often miss*: lesser-known and little-practiced gems of real cultural change in action. Our research is not academic: It's based on real actions from successful leaders and change agents – whether they are managers or individual contributors (both can be leaders). They hail from all walks of life. Through their stories, we hope you can find *your* way. Out of respect for their privacy, we have chosen not to use real names of people or companies we have worked with.

Maybe you are leading inside a big corporation, a community church, a nonprofit, or a small family business. Maybe you are a teacher, professor, doctor, or owner of a daycare center. Maybe you are simply a person with a desire and curiosity to make things a little bit better in your world.

Whoever you are … if you want new ways to steer your boat in a storm …

This book is for you.

SUMMARY
of Introduction

Expert change and innovation is demanded of leaders today amid "a perfect storm" of constantly shifting conditions.

Growing a Fit Culture is the solution for leaders to help organizations speed up and compete better.

There are simple, small changes you can make to become more fit.

Whether you are a leader who wants to improve the health of your organization's culture or you are facing a mission critical strategic shift and are concerned about it "sticking" – this book is for you.

Overview: 9 Truths from Nature for Fit Cultures

Drawing from discoveries in recent fields of advanced Neuroscience, Evolutionary Theory, and Anthropology, this book defines nine fundamental truths from nature and applies them to building a stronger culture that is more fit to compete in a fast-moving economy, as well being more, fulfilling and fit to work in for employees and managers.

I. CREATE: The Foundation

Chapter 1: **The Seed is the Tree … or a Dandelion**. In nature, everything has a clear purpose to fulfill, encoded in its seed. In business, you must be intentional in reminding people of the clear purpose behind activity, to avoid it becoming random or bureaucratic.

Chapter 2: Vision - Fire Lights the Way. In nature, movement typically follows the path of least resistance. In business, movement forward catches on through a shared vision: the fire of motivation.

Chapter 3: **Trust is like the Sun**. In nature, the sun is the source of all life. In business, trust is the essential energy in which lasting growth occurs, continuously. The ultimate workplace is one where 100% trust is completely assumed.

II. GROW Through Cultivation

Chapter 4: The Structure of Growth - Boundaries, Governance, and Guardrails. In nature, structure and rules interact perfectly with dynamic, constant change. In business, structure and governance need to create collaborative, empowered, and self-accountable workplaces: That leads to better results both in the soft elements of the business (people) and in the hard results (ROI).

Chapter 5: Collaborate: Power up the Tribe! In nature, everything interacts as part of a system – fruitful harvests are the end of the chain. In business, boundaries across the chains must be dissolved to foster interaction and cooperation. This allows faster adaptability.

Chapter 6: Communication: Water Always Flows. In nature, communication flows like water – endless, non-stop, and essential for life. In business, communication is the life force of profit and wealth, but must flow more naturally – leaders need to build bridges and break down dams behind which meaning and information are often stuck.

III. EVOLVE Through Learning

Chapter 7: Learning: How Nature Avoids Extinction. Nature uses learning to avoid extinction. In business, building a learning culture is the remedy to support an environment of sustainable growth.

Chapter 8: Mindsets: Navigating the Icebergs. In nature, the truth may not be obvious or easy to spot – such as icebergs. In business, mindsets are the hidden force of our thinking that keep us stuck or help us change when progress is needed.

Chapter 9: Procreate: Spread Leadership DNA. In nature, survival is about passing on your DNA. In business, leaders are the carriers of DNA and need to see a fundamental part of their job as passing it on to the next generation.

The Best Way to Use This Book

Each chapter in this book is designed to stand on its own – like nine short essays that provide unique insight and suggestions for building a great culture.

And the book as a whole can be a comprehensive approach to building a more adaptive culture.

We recommend that you stop trying to super-size leadership and change.

In the case of change, bigger is *not* better.

Choose one or two practices that personally resonate for you, that stretch you, and do them consistently.

Small change is the evolutionary way to have a lasting impact.

Create the Foundation
(Chapters 1-3)

The first truth we explore from nature is what establishes a healthy system. Nothing in nature can sustain, evolve or grow without a catalyzing force that infuses it with energy – that provides a solid foundation for growth. In the business world, this is expressed through a leader's intention, vision, and the presence of trust.

Through stories of a local Starbucks trying to win the designation "world's fastest service" or a law firm formed with the intention to create a great place to work (which happens to make money too), we illustrate how a strong foundation can be built from a passionate idea.

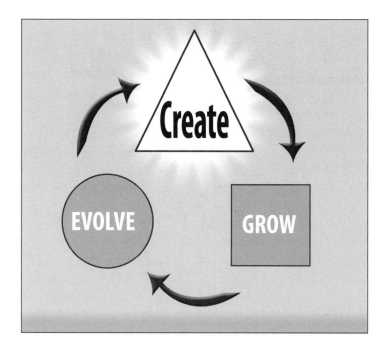

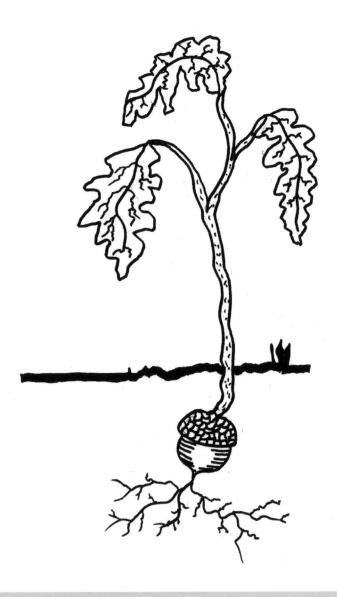

Chapter One: INTENTION
The Seed Is the Tree (or a Dandelion)

In Chapter 1, we explore "Why intention?" People bring passionate energy to what they are inspired by – and passion is what drives commitment: the foundation of a healthy culture. You can call it engagement, call it involvement, call it empowerment – it's the essential "seed" that creates the tree.

The Seed Is the Tree (or a Dandelion)

Nature's Truth #1:

In nature, everything has a clear
purpose to fulfill, encoded in its seed.

In business, you must be intentional in reminding
people of the clear purpose behind activity, to
avoid it becoming random or bureaucratic.

*"The way to gain a good reputation is to
endeavor to be what you desire to appear."*

— Socrates

June 2005 was when the bottom dropped out.

We had been working non-stop training and coaching leaders for a combined total of 40 years. One day we came to the end of a 10-year run of a very busy stage of work, and there was no "next thing" on the horizon.

During the two years which followed, a very, very small number of projects came our way. This was puzzling, given we had worked with hundreds of clients who claimed we had changed the course of their lives and businesses. In our industry, boutique firm marketing is primarily based on referral. Having been in business together for over a decade, we wondered what it meant that referrals had dried up. We did the conferences, the articles, the phone calls. We made a few key strategic shifts, resulting in more than our fair share of distractions and missteps. At a few low points, we entertained a host of alternatives – for example, opening a burrito stand (as a talented cook, Gerry felt this could be a simpler and more satisfying way to serve people).

During this time, Lisa – the single head of household – faced a series of wrenching personal changes, including the traumatic death of her father. Our support circle felt sympathy for the plight we were going through, but didn't know what to do. Some grew more distant, not knowing how to support – maybe concerned our lack of success might rub off. Most suggested to us both at some point, "Perhaps you should consider a new career." (Watching how people respond when someone they care about is sinking is a very important lesson in compassion.)

No matter what we did, we seemed to be caught in our version of a perfect storm: a combination of misreading key trends in our field; lack of "luck" in business development efforts; and a growing trend to replace what we do with internal organizational development staff.

We gave thorough consideration to important questions like: "What is the true value and service we are meant to bring to others?" "Do we *really* want to do this work, in this way?" "What does it mean to be invested in the change efforts of our clients, but not care too much?" "What can we do to maximize our true talents and minimize our weaknesses (i.e., partner with someone who already has client relationships)? Still, the "magic bullet" answer remained elusive.

When faced with relentless worldly evidence that is contrary to your core purpose and vision…when everyone around you is questioning your ability and judgment, where do you turn for answers? What do you place your trust in?

The answer in our situation was both unlikely and obvious, marked by the tiny presence of a nagging, persistent voice that never stopped or let up: "Keep going. This IS your work. There is a need for new ways of developing leaders, for different ways of doing business in turbulent times. You have to help people discover it."

Through the doubt, the crises, and the questions, what kept us from giving up? We expanded our definition of success, changed how we delivered our work, simplified our finances, and became more humble and empathetic to the challenges our clients face every day.

We came to see each obstacle – frustrating as it was – as a reminder of our responsibility to make this business work. We came to see that for us to serve clients who faced unrelenting change, risk, and challenge, we had to do so ourselves. Weathering our own storms helped bring into clear focus both how we define success for ourselves AND what we are not willing to do. Teaching and leadership is our purpose. The only true failure would be in giving up.

It forced honesty. Clarity of intention. And deeply personal lessons about change and adaptability.

It was our seed. It was our commitment.

Intention Is the Seed of Everything.

Everything is the product of its seed.

While "intention" is the most abstract concept we approach in this book, it is the most important. You cannot grow a powerful oak tree from a dandelion seed.

When the culmination of a person's history, values, and personal passion intersects with a significant opportunity or problem, the seeds of greatness are germinated.

Where Does Greatness Begin?

Proper attention to the starting point of anything is a crucial predictor of its success or failure. This can be as small as a meeting or as big as a new business venture.

Too often, leaders barrel ahead with tasks and goals in business without being aware of their real intention – also known as commitment. Change efforts in today's organizations are often a "dog-chasing-tail" problem. The executive decides on an improvement to grow the business or cut costs. His commitment is driven by pressure from the boss for quarterly numbers and awareness that his bonus is at stake – along with his career trajectory. The executive throws the responsibility to implement it "over the fence" to the next layer in the hierarchy – the managers. Possibly with a business case that frames how it will "help us serve our customers better" (but maybe not…and even if that exists, nobody *really* believes that's the true intention). Then, the managers are left to figure out how to translate the meaning of this latest "good idea" into employee commitment. Doing this initiative will most likely threaten several jobs, and while nobody is talking about that element, employees aren't idiots.

Six months later, executives wonder why the efforts at training and implementing the change have not realized the cost reductions or growth predictions. Confused and facing increasing pressure, they move to one of the Big-Three tools in their kit: Layoffs (or reorganization resulting in layoffs). Program freezes. Budget cuts. (In one organization we worked with, the first program to be cut was a company-wide initiative based on the popular Stephen M. Covey book *The Speed of Trust*.)

The mixed messages of "growth, personal accountability, serving our customers" versus "decisions about cuts with little input from those affected" can be traced to the original quality of the commitment: the seed. In an organizational context, the most powerful intentions – those that drive sustainable growth and success over the long haul, address three important questions:

1) Are leaders *conscious and transparent* about their intention?
   (Do people know WHY you are doing what you're doing?)

2) Does it *serve* something larger than the need for money or
   power?

3) Will it make the business – or world – better?

The bigger the "Yes!" to these three questions, the bigger the potential for growth – and the more fruitful the harvest. Whether adopting a new software program, reforming healthcare, or running a strategy session – the quality of the "seed" will determine the fruit – its quality, its form, and the timing of its harvest.

High potential "seeds" – i.e., ideas – draw committed people and foster trust. This helps them grow stronger and faster. Seeds planted from self-serving or small interests such as greed, fear, or power are like weeds – they suck resources from the soil and choke out fruit-bearing plants.

To further complicate matters, advances in the field of neuro-science (which we describe in depth in Chapter 3, "Trust Is Like the Sun") show precisely where and how our brain detects the nature and quality of people's intentions, whether or not they are stated. Even if you fool yourself into believing you are serving a higher agenda with a self-serving intention, people will know the difference. There is a brain structure inside us that is dedicated to just such detection: It's called spindle cells. These help you gauge whether someone is trustworthy or not – and does it within seconds.

Ever heard of Minute Clinic? They are at the front end of a fascinating wave of healthcare reform called "healthcare retail." It all began when Rick Krieger endured a 3-hour emergency room visit for his son's sore throat in 1999. One thousand people would have sat in that waiting room and had different responses to the experience – but Rick saw opportunity. His Eureka! moment didn't stop with fleeting annoyance at the ridiculous time involved in a strep throat culture. Rick recognized it as the seed of an entire crop of new ways of delivering healthcare. After this experience, he began to wonder: "Why isn't there a quick and convenient way to get treatment for simple medical problems?" This seed turned into the launch of a handful of nurse-practitioner clinics, inside Cub Foods in the Minneapolis area, to treat basic medical issues during retail store hours. Two years later, after overcoming gigantic obstacles and a buyout, CVS Caremark – the largest retail pharmacy in the United States with 6,000 retail and specialty stores in 43 states in 2007 – will ensure that Minute Clinic's bright kiosks and unprecedented customer service will be nearly everywhere.

Even if you don't have a dream to revolutionize healthcare – or anything else – you can sow powerful seeds in a venue as simple as your weekly staff meeting. One of our clients is a senior executive in a major pharmaceutical company. Even though this isn't a strategy for everyone, at the time we worked with him, he began every meeting with mystical poetry reading. He planned the reading to illustrate a relevant issue, theme, or problem the group was struggling with. By the way; he is one of the most effective leaders we've known.

Keep walking, though there's no place to get to
Don't try to see through the distances
That's not for human beings
Move within
But don't move the way fear makes you move.

— **From The Illuminated Rumi, 1997, translation by Coleman Barks**

Be clear what you want. Plant your seed carefully. Tend it without fear.

Cultivating the Seed

Every seed has an encoded DNA: A dandelion seed will never become an oak tree.

And, every seed has the *potential* to achieve its destiny (but not every seed grows).

Having observed and studied great leadership for several decades, we have noticed that intentions (seeds) of seemingly equal promise create remarkably different results. An idea or concept succeeds brilliantly in one situation, and the same strategy falls completely flat the next time. The promising acquisition looked *so* good on paper, but in reality it became a nightmare – draining people's energy and morale and choking the promised growth projections.

Too often, in the zeal to grow, little attention is paid to the environment in which you are planting the "growth opportunity." Lisa's gardener recently told her

"I spend most of my time preparing the soil. I let my clients know that so they're not wondering why the results don't show visibly, sooner. My neighbors used to knock on my door and ask why my plants were bigger and healthier than theirs. Nothing died in my garden. The secret was taking the time to prepare great soil – that's the process that allows a plant to grow to its full potential. The quality of the plant is important, but the soil is the environment in which it thrives or withers." In the Colorado foothills, most soil is hard clay…not a conducive environment for planting and growth. It struck Lisa that this is exactly parallel to an organization's culture. Too often growth opportunities and talented people are struggling in hard-packed soil that is not prepared for the challenges it must endure: the systems, processes, structure, and communication practices are often not set up to support dynamic, fast-moving strategies and constant change.

This is culture: It is the soil for your seed.

What does the alignment between seed quality, soil preparation, planting, and cultivating mean in action? Lisa met Derek in a business community roundtable in Denver. She was struck by the alignment of his intention, his actions, and the results he created, having planted and cultivated the seed of a "law firm that transforms the way legal work is done."

Derek's Story

In 2001, Derek was seven years into his career as a top merger and acquisition lawyer for a Colorado branch of a national law firm, having launched his career in NY at one of the top 10 firms for "deal-makers." He relates the story of how he left it behind to build his vision of a different way to practice law. We share it with you here, as a powerful reminder of the importance of intention.

"As a lawyer, I was always different. I was trained as a traditional lawyer but I grew up in our family business; we owned a furniture retailer and a bicycle retailer, and I started working for the business at age 11. Later, I got my undergraduate degree in business.

I always saw myself not just as someone providing legal services, but in the business of creating satisfied customers. Our family furniture business put food on the table and put me through college not because we sold a reclining chair to one customer. We sold a recliner; we made a customer happy; they came back and bought a kitchen table and chairs. Later, they came for a living room set, still later they came for a bedroom set.

It's pretty easy to figure out how to build a business by delivering value to your customers.

Throughout my career I paid close attention to how the "business of law" worked. How the office was set up. How interpersonal relationships worked between employees. How the business interacted effectively with its customers. Most lawyers don't ever think about these aspects of their job – it's definitely not taught in law school, and lawyers are not trained to take the client's perspective. On many occasions during deals, I felt like I was "in the middle," bridging a gap between lawyers and businesspeople. I had a knack for understanding what clients were saying and needing in plain English.

One of the central issues that bothered me about the legal world was the financial structure. Most of the largest national firms – considered to be the most successful law firms – are still operating on a business model founded around the time of World War II. They have a pyramid structure, are slow to adopt technology, and their fee structures incent inefficiency. The billable hour as a measure of service and payment was a way to offload the risk of inevitable variances in projects (a reasonable premise for a service business), but it has created a perverse incentive. The more inefficient a lawyer is (as long as the client doesn't complain), the more money the lawyer makes. The potential of attorneys being rewarded for being inefficient struck me as antithetical to providing the best service to clients.

From the side of the employee, a top performer in a national firm is typically paid the same as a bottom performer of the same seniority. The only data most people inside large law firms know about you are your "stats"

– based on billable hours. The most highly prized lawyers billed the most hours. They were the best worker-bees), but they were often not the best lawyers. Bottom line, firms were unwittingly hoisting some of the worst legal talent on their best clients.

I spent a lot of time thinking, "There must be a better way." Law firms in general are not change-friendly places, so I knew I would not have a receptive audience for my ideas. Finally, one day in 2001, the impetus came for me to act on my years of thinking.

In 2001, the firm was suffering from the dot-com bust and only one corporate associate made partner in a firm of 900+ attorneys. I had concerns about the firm's ability to grow in Colorado (a necessity for more partners to be added in the Colorado office) and had little confidence in the leadership in the Colorado office. In fact, I became famous for remarking to my colleagues at one point: "The partners don't know what the %&# they are doing." In order to deal with the firm's economic issues resulting from the dot-com bust (too many lawyers without enough work), the firm offered voluntary buy-out packages to employees. I opted to take the money and run in December of 2001. The buy-out money gave me the capital I needed to start my own firm in the beginning of 2002. I felt much more comfortable betting on my own abilities than staking my future on the management team of the Colorado office. At the time I made my decision, I kept recalling a random quote I had seen at the bottom of an e-mail once: "The weak quit and stay put; the strong quit and move on."

In hindsight, I was absolutely right in doubting the prospects of the Colorado office. Within two years of my departure, the entire firm broke apart. I understand some of the partners may still be mired in lawsuits related to the demise of the firm.

Everyone thought I was crazy to start a business in 2002 with the uncertain economy, but I know that when things are less certain – that's when people are open to change. I chose to found my firm on two specific premises:

(1) Create a better environment for lawyers to work in. Develop a fair compensation scheme for everyone who works at the firm and make sure it is based on merit and contribution, not based on title and seniority. This eradicates the stratified class system that (i) is typical of big firms, and (ii) results in a less friendly work environment. (I am a big believer in looking at the incentives in a deal – if you look at the incentives you learn a lot about why people act the way they do.)

My belief was this: If you treat employees fairly and with respect, they'll be happier, and that will accomplish two things: (i) Retention of good employees, who, in turn, help you recruit the best candidates—the system feeds on itself; and (ii) Happy employees who provide good service to your clients. And, happy clients recommend your service to others. It's a sustainable model that can grow; and everyone wins.

(2) Create a better model to deliver service to the client. Consumers of legal services are not getting what they need and want, due to a financial model and archaic administrative practices. For me, the goal was for employees to earn a good living and for clients to receive top-notch legal services they considered to be a good value. We constructed a firm based on the most productive assets a law firm can have, and provided a different environment to succeed. We hire people who are experienced (already trained in national law firms) and technologically adept, and remove the administrative burden. Instead of three administrative pass-throughs for every document change, if I'm negotiating a document on a conference call, I make changes real time. The client asks "[David], when can you have a revised draft to me?" I'd say – "Are you in front of your computer? I'll send it to you right now." We focus on less waste, on project-based and fixed-fee billing, and monthly retainers where clients can budget and call any time to get all their questions answered.

Has it worked?

- In 2008, we were selected by Denver Business Journal as "Best Place to Work in Denver" in our category. Not many law firms make that list!

- We started in 2002 with one lawyer and have grown to 11 lawyers... and counting! In 2009 and 2010, in the midst of the "Great Recession" when most firms reduced corporate groups by 20%, we hired attorneys.

- The majority of clients are referred to us by other clients.

One of our top private investors told me recently:

I've never worked with a lawyer like you. Working with you has completely changed my perception of what lawyers are. You are practical. Every time I pay my legal bills, I feel like I got a good deal.

I am proud of what we have accomplished. We said we could do it better, and our clients and the community have validated it: We're doing the work right and making the customers happy."

No question that Derek planted the right seed, has worked at preparing his soil (culture), and cultivates its growth by thinking always about the initial purpose and how he can best enable it in his law firm.

Will Your Seed Grow...Or Wither?

We've all heard the wisdom: "A mediocre idea well-executed will outperform a great idea poorly executed." In our experience, *both* the idea *and* the execution are of equal importance: You don't need home-run ideas every time, but the quality of the original idea is very relevant. And unless the leader's intention can draw commitment in the form of a host of gardeners, there will be no harvest.

What makes the difference in two "oak tree" seeds planted, where one thrives and one dies?

Based on research and decades of working with leaders – we have defined two personal attributes leaders can cultivate in themselves to ensure they are planting their best seeds (intentions) in good soil. We will explore them in more detail in Chapter 9 – but are planting the seeds of the ideas here.

1) Self-Awareness.

In February 2007, Harvard Business Review featured an article *Discovering Your Authentic Leadership* [9] reporting that the key to great leadership is authenticity. In the largest in-depth study of leadership development ever undertaken, the authors asked: "How can people become and remain authentic leaders?"

The study singled out leaders who achieved superior results over a sustained period of time, and showed that self-aware leaders demonstrate two important change-friendly qualities:

- **Transparency**. They examine and craft their life story in a way others can relate to, to show how they have been tested, overcome adversity, and exercised courage. (Whether written or not, *you* have a life story). Great leaders also use their own setbacks to identify their core values and principles, which they don't waver from when tested. This is also how they become fearless – so great intentions become great deeds, versus being degraded by the fear of approval or failure. They understand that a satisfying life is less about "rewards" on the outside and more about the character you cultivate on the inside. This takes a commitment beyond simply knowing it's important.

- **Surrounded by Strength.** They hire people smarter than themselves. They choose highly trustworthy confidants who can do what they cannot. The self-aware leader knows his or her strengths and weaknesses, accepts that he or she is not perfect, and looks for people who can fill in the gaps. These folks may be personal advisors or members of their team. Weak leaders hire people they *like*. Courageous leaders often hire people they *don't* like *because* they bring a different point of view. Either way, the authentic leader is both confident and humble enough to know they can't turn a seed into an oak tree by themselves.

2) Commitment.

When the going gets rough (which it always does over the long haul), how strongly do you stay connected to where it all began? When passion for your purpose is greater than the challenges you face, your commitment will cultivate the seed into its best expression.

There may be a collective hunger for the harvest (how many people have sat in emergency waiting rooms and wished what Rick Krieger of the Minute Clinic did?) but a leader's commitment – symbolically and practically – drives his or her willingness to persevere.

The reason most efforts to lead change fail can be traced to too few seeds planted in weak or harsh soil, with expectations of instant growth or harvest. Some leaders toss their seed over the fence and hope it grows in someone else's yard. Others don't tend the seed once planted. Self-discipline means staying engaged, even when you don't want to. Even when the plan falls apart. Even when the adversity becomes unbearable.

After Thomas Edison's seven-hundredth unsuccessful attempt to invent the electric light, he was asked by a *New York Times* reporter, "How does it feel to have failed seven hundred times?" The great inventor responded: "I have not failed seven hundred times. I have not failed once. I have succeeded in proving those seven hundred ways will not work. When I have eliminated the ways that will not work, I will find the way that will work." Edison finally found the one that would work, and invented the electric light.

When Rick Krieger "invented" retail healthcare, he faced tremendous opposition from doctors and traditional healthcare institutions that felt the only safe treatment came from physicians. He held the intention and found a way – even after all 14 venture capitalist investors abandoned ship.

The antidote for the forces that test you is clear intention. The formula is simple, even if not easy. (And it helps if you surround yourself with people who remind you of your intentions from time to time, in a positive way.)

Start with healthy seeds and soil.

Cultivate commitment – yours and theirs.

Reap the harvest.

SUMMARY
Nature's Truth #1:

In nature, everything has a clear purpose to fulfill, encoded in its seed.

In business, you must be intentional in reminding people of the clear purpose behind activity to avoid it becoming random or bureaucratic.

To ensure your change efforts have a strong start, address three important questions:

1) **Are you conscious and transparent about why you are doing what you're doing?**

2) **Does it serve someone besides yourself?**

3) **Will it make the business – or world – better?**

Leaders can cultivate powerful intentions by improving:

1) **Self-awareness** – the ability to learn from adversity and tests.

2) **Commitment** – the will to return to your intention and keep going, and surround yourself with people who will help remind you.

Making It Work! Small Changes for Developing Your Intention

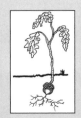

Here are a few practices for setting powerful intention:

1) **Quiet mind**. You need a regular practice to quiet the busy-ness of your mind. A mind that is incapable of rest has no room for new ideas and insights. Ideally, meditate daily, even if it's just for a few minutes. Just find the method you will do regularly: for some it's yoga or pick-up basketball. For others it's prayer and church. For still others it's painting or playing music. A colleague of mine has an aerial studio in her backyard, and climbs to practice the art of trapeze.

2) **Meta-intention**. Great leaders have an intention to do something great, that serves. The ultimate intention is to find a pathway to make a difference and a contribution. What is that for you?

3) **Play**. Research proves that the balance between work and play drives better innovation. Regular open space for fun and games will make it more likely the seeds of greatness will arrive in a steady stream at your doorstep. According to a recent interview of one of Apple's technologists, the way they solve the big software problems involves lots of play. "We have a ping pong table, a pool table and a basketball court next to our programming work rooms. When the programmers have hit a block, they outline the issues, then play a very competitive session of hoops, or one of the other games, for a while. When one of the programmers has an insight, they call out a signal, and everyone stops playing and gathers at the conference table. They then outline a solution to the current problem and everyone writes code for 4 or 5 hours. If they get stuck doing that, they go back to play and the cycle repeats.

4) **Symbol**. A common coaching exercise for someone who is trying to strengthen an intention is to affirm it through a visual reminder every day. While I (Gerry) have had many exciting sports cars in my life, more recently the garage has contained only the practical kind that haul lots of people, sheets of plywood and my two boats. Recently, and with the prompting of my car-happy and very influential son, I've found myself again craving a 996 (for the uninitiated, that's a 1999 – 2002 Porsche 911 Carrera). I printed a picture of the model and color I have in mind and it sits right above my business phone and is in my line of sight daily. By the time you are reading these words, it will be under my house. That's the power of intention.

Chapter Two: VISION
Fire Lights the Way

In Chapter 2, we explore what makes the concept of vision motivating and real for people, and how you can boost the power of where you are going in a way that people can connect to. This process doesn't need to be based on a grand "save-the-world" vision. It's simply the "fire" that motivates people.

Fire Lights the Way

Nature's Truth #2:

In nature, movement typically follows
the path of least resistance.

In business, movement forward is
catalyzed by shared vision:

It is the fire of motivation.

*"The future belongs to those who see possibilities
before they become obvious."*

— John Scully, former CEO of Apple

Vision. One of those over-used, cliché, and often-misunderstood terms in business (which is why we feel it deserves another hearing).

Vision is not about the pieces of paper that return from the off-site meeting at the resort. Vision is the discussion that happened around the pieces of paper.

Vision is not a consultant's exercise to co-mingle a senior team's goals. Vision is the experience that "fused" the goals.

Vision is not the posters with each word birthed through hours of agonizing debate. Vision is the commitment the debate fostered.

Vision is a simple concept and should be *expressed* simply.

Vision is an idea backed by emotion: a clear, compelling image.

One that answers: What do we want? How can we make things better? What's possible?

Most definitions of leadership assume you want to take people to a place they aren't already. The question a leader must address is "Why would anyone want to follow me?" The answer lives in your vision – a visible and powerful statement of your passion.

That's it.

If you take a vacation, you have an image in your mind of the experience you want: An idea in picture or movie form. That image shapes your decisions, choices, experiences, and thoughts along the way – whether or not you are conscious of it. (Research shows that most of the time, you're not.) You attempt to create the vacation that "matches" the movie – or become unhappy when it doesn't. Sometimes you veer off course. Sometimes spontaneity was part of the vision. For most people, planning a vacation creates a sense of motivation and urgency: There is a specific date when it will happen and a destination (or a concept of an experience you want to have). It marks time and provides something to look forward to. It raises the spirits and builds anticipation – for yourself and, if you are part of a family or group, for others who will be going. It assumes personal responsibility: While you may hire a tour guide you don't expect them to *make* your vacation a great experience. By the stories you tell, the websites you visit, the books you read – you create the experience you want, even before you leave. Sitting around the dinner table, you might share possible outings and experiences you want to have.

Paradoxically, when you are present to each moment, you can appreciate and fully enjoy the planning, anticipation, and journey of getting *to* the vacation. Making the journey fun is the magic of a great vision, and can energize us to seek new experiences, not avoid them. In the workplace, after we have been through a large, *successful* change, vision can create greater capacity and acceptance for more change.

This description is analogous to the process of creating vision for a team or organization during change, or in any situation in which you want to energize people toward something new.

During vacation, you will experience new things (change), and the anticipation and emotional connection for that change is usually positive – in part, because YOU have chosen to be in it. Further, most people say the best part of the vacation often happens in the small, unexpected moments along the journey – like finding a fruit stand with fresh mango, having an unplanned interaction with a unique local person or family, or encountering a beautiful animal in the wild or in the sea. It is often the natural, small moments and relationships that weave the fabric of a great vacation.

On vacation, it's not expected that everyone will have the same experience at the same time, or that every experience will be equally fun, interesting, or uplifting. That's also true in an organization or team. On a great vacation, each person has some accountability and freedom to create the vacation experience they want. A good leader will ensure his or her vision does this for the team.

Without an adventure or change in routine, the fire of excitement can die down into a low-level burn of routine and daily minutiae disconnected from purpose. As a leader, it's important to stoke the fire of anticipation and newness by creating a challenge or goal that energizes people. (See "A Coffee Dream" at the end of this chapter.) Vision doesn't have to be grandiose. It should stretch people and bring out their best, not create panic, apathy, burnout, or the desire to give up.

Like a vacation, a shared vision can help leaders define time, create anticipation, catalyze a common set of stories, build relationships, and create a unifying experience for new, out-of-the-ordinary experiences.

Vision is the unique gift of the human experience. In its most fantastic expression, it is the line between what we can imagine and what we can create. It is the reason Michelangelo's work is still revered to this day. It is the reason Dorothy's journey to Oz remains a cultural icon of the blurry line between fantasy and reality (and why the new theatrical production *Wicked*, a charming tale of the "backstory" of the *Wizard of Oz*, is so wildly popular).

Vision is a fire in YOU to create and express something that makes the world a little bit better. Stoke it and you create a bonfire. Starve the fire and it dies out (or goes rogue without your guidance). If you want others to be part of your vision, you need a way to pass the torch – so each person can own a piece of the fire.

Vision is the light by which ideas are illuminated into reality. During change, leaders have a tremendous responsibility to carry the torch of the vision and remind people of it often. Otherwise, their ideas – and the revenues that chase them – turn into a cold pile of bureaucratic processes: meaningless activity that is disconnected from its purpose.

And remember this about vision: People will have a very hard time letting go of a past – even one that is not good for them – if they can't see a better future.

Creating Urgency for Change

"One of the top predictors of success in leading change is whether or not there is adequate Urgency."[10]

The very words "urgency" and "change" can trigger strong responses in people: "We don't want people running around with their hair on fire." Lisa was brought into a consulting situation recently where the lead consultant told her that she couldn't use the word "urgency" because of the client's negative reaction. Curiously, they have been working to embed a vision and strategy for change for about three years and, in that time, very little meaningful traction has been gained toward the desired changes - even by the consultant's estimation. Hum?

Urgency is simply a reflection of adequate motivation. It's the gas that drives the car. You can move the car without fuel. But how far and how fast depends on having fuel.

If a vision for the future is well-developed, people will be drawn into its promise and will find their *own* commitment to its activities. The goal of finding the urgency behind your vision is to fuel the motivation that leads to commitment.

Think about your personal efforts to change: eating better, losing a few pounds, getting in shape . . . . Aren't you more likely to be motivated when you have some sense of urgency?

When Gerry's Dad turned 47, he talked about feeling an impending doom – the imminent milestone of "hitting the BIG 5-0." His response to his aging crisis was to suddenly decide to resurrect his tennis game – which he dropped a couple of decades earlier given his focus on raising two boys and earning a living. His vision was to play in the Long Island Open Tennis Tournament eight months later – and compete well. He said, "I just want to play really well, and not be humiliated playing a bunch of young guys." He had not done anything remotely related to working out since he was in the Army in his late teens. (He claimed to hate exercise, although he loved tennis.) Throughout the entire winter and spring leading up to the tournament, Dad would come home from work, run to the local high school track, and run a few miles around it (usually in the dark). Apparently his "urgency" to compete well was high!

He won the tournament, beating a 19-year-old university student who was nationally ranked in the finals.

Are You Motivating or Mandating Change?

Earlier we related a fact that many people survive heart attacks, but most cardiac surgery patients soon resume their old ways. Only about 20% give up smoking, change their diet, or get more exercise.

If you remember only one thing about change, remember that it is a CHOICE – and that if you are leading a team or organization, you must help each individual commit to that choice.

That commitment is strongest when aimed both toward something people want and away from something they can clearly see should be avoided.

The Secret behind Maximum Motivation

"A crisis is a terrible thing to waste"

— **Dick Clark, CEO, Merck, speaking about their recovery from the Vioxx crisis.**

Urgency is a state of maximum motivation.

Humans are hard wired to be motivated by just two factors: (1) Towards goals, a vision, things we want and desire; and (2) Away from danger or things we want to avoid, prevent and stop. While everyone has both kinds of motivation, we also have a preference for one over the other. Why do you brush your teeth? One person focuses on how clean, smooth and good their teeth feel [towards motivation]. Another person will say it's to avoid decay and trips to the dentist [away from motivation]. We can all relate to both descriptions, but typically what drives you to behave is more like a hierarchy of preferences. Because we all respond to both directions of motivation, if leaders want to create maximum motivation, they must construct their story and vision using both concepts. This leads to more engagement, commitment, ownership, and energy.

Your tendency will be to talk about your vision using the words that *you* most respond to: either towards or away from. By using both, you will align with a wider range of people and create more motivation.

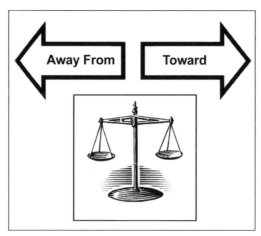

Try this simple exercise:

1) Notice what about your vision can be described as "towards" motivation factors: "We will achieve . . ." "You will benefit by . . ." "The results will be . . ." Write down these words.

2) Notice what about your vision can be described as "away from" motivation factors: "We will avoid . . ." "You can prevent . . ." "The vision will stop (something bad) from happening . . ." Write down these words.

3) The next time you are talking to someone, sprinkle both of these throughout your conversation, and watch what they respond to. That provides clues to their motivation.

There's another reason to consciously tap both sides of human motivation: The strength of motivation is the antidote for the inevitable fear of any change – which everyone has to face in order to accomplish something they have never done. Too often, leaders allow fear (of failure, feedback, criticism) "small thinking," or the challenge of obstacles to dampen their resolve. Concern about taking risks that could adversely affect this quarter's profits or a boss' or board's perception of their value becomes a constant drip-drip-drip of water that dampens great ideas. "We don't have time." "We don't have room for that investment in our plan right now." "What's the expected ROI?" "What will Wall Street say?"

The stronger the case for the change – the greater the collective urgency for the change. The greater the urgency, the more fuel you have to drive forward with bold steps.

Remember Bill and Dan from our Introduction, who likened the task of leading a major organizational change to "extreme skiing?" Neither of them considered failure an option. The stakes are high, the company's future rests on getting it right and, as a result, there is tremendous excitement, energy, and pull toward a better future. In this case, the failures of the past, circumstances of the present, and a huge future opportunity have aligned to create a perfect setup for maximum motivation: the urgency for real change.

Banging the Drum: Storytelling and Fire

Once you have the urgency for real change, how do you translate that motivation into widespread action? What does it take to encourage people to join up, to buy-in, to commit? In one sense, that is what the rest of this book is about. In another sense, vision itself is a fire: While the initial flame begins with one leader, unless it's a personal achievement, it goes nowhere until the leader figures out how to get others to build it into a bonfire.

One powerful element of fanning the vision fire has its roots in an ancient ritual of human experience through the ages: storytelling. This is not just a bedtime ritual for small children anymore! Leaders who beat the odds at implementing change use the power of story to create emotional commitment.

Prometheus, best known as the Greek "God of Fire," is a great example. As a champion of humankind known for his wily intelligence, he stole fire from Zeus and gave it to mortals. The remarkable and interesting fact about this myth is that every major indigenous culture has a version of it: Native Americans, the Vedas from Hinduism, Chinese lore, the list goes on. (And these stories emerged around the same period – long before the Internet and Wikipedia.)

There is richness to the fire-stealing myth on many levels: Given the power and rarity of fire, it was extremely important and desirable among tribes. The invention of fire allowed human beings several luxuries, including the ability to continue activity into the night; to protect themselves from predators (non-primate animals don't usually come near fire); and a way to cook food that was more digestible. If the fire went out, you were doomed.

Your story need not be as universal as fire stealing myths, but it should tap into the emotional response we all have to a relevant and compelling story.

The Future Is Hard to See

"If you limit your choices only to what seems possible or reasonable, you disconnect yourself from what you truly want. All that is left is a compromise."

— **Robert Fritz**

In creating more adaptable organizations, we don't recommend setting off fire alarms in the building. We offer the "fire-stealing" metaphor as a powerful analogy for a leader's ability to hold the vision for people in a way that provides illumination, protection, and "digestible" stories about why we are doing what we do. All wrapped inside a story of sufficient urgency as an alarm to counter complacency and overcome resistance to change.

Leaders who want adaptable teams and companies need to see their job as shining light in places where there is confusion or darkness. The reason that people tend to focus on the past and on problems, is because they have a memory of them – they're known. The future is harder to grasp. Leaders who do a good job of creating a clear, unambiguous definition of "what we want," "where we're going," and "what we are avoiding," will find more people around them focused on building that future.

This is *not* a fluffy or esoteric concept reserved for industries in the creative realm. Stories penetrate our consciousness and capture our attention all day long: the media back-story to the championship tennis tournament … or tragic family loss. Remember Joanie Rochette? Joannie skated for an Olympic medal two days after her mother died unexpectedly of a heart attack. Remember the tremendous emotional connection those of us who watched felt to her? In an age of reality TV, people's life stories have become a vicarious way to tap into and experience the stories of our own lives. But stories have been mysteriously eradicated as a communication medium in business (other than at the watercooler or before the meeting starts) – a hold-over, we guess, from a fairly recent time when it was deemed "unnecessary" for people to use their brains at work.

In fact, the preferred methods for communicating and convincing people of an idea – through predictive analysis, logic, "the numbers," and a focus on efficiency and productivity -- have dominated the business world only since the late 19th century. Author Peter Drucker says the man who started it all had as much impact on our modern world as Sigmund Freud and Charles Darwin. Frederick Winslow Taylor, the inventor of "Scientific Management," was a Bethlehem Steel employee who invented early efficiency methods (such as time/motion studies) that led to the achievement of huge gains in the productivity of workers – at the same time that the worker's empowerment was displaced by managers holding clipboards. Since that time, his influence still permeates the way we work today, and is at the root of how we design organizations, define jobs, measure performance, incent people – and even affects how we decide new programs. It's also behind the rising number of hours we believe we have to work, accompanied by the nagging feeling that it's never enough. Carrying a BlackBerry and checking email on Sunday are evidence that Peter Drucker wasn't exaggerating the impact of Taylor's Scientific Management on the way we work and live.

All this is not saying that productivity and efficiency are unimportant. But, they are not *sufficient* methods by themselves for leading and adapting to the overwhelming pace of change in today's work world. It's time to bring back balance of both sides of the brain – analytical AND emotional. Productivity connected *to* a compelling, meaningful purpose.

In fact, recent research from brain scans and neuro-science – as well as our own innate wisdom – provide proof that fact-based considerations represent only a small element of a person's decision or commitment. Because human beings have free will and aren't robots, we can decide whether to respond to change and, if so, how. At the core of what motivates anyone to make a change, regardless of whether it's small or big, is a motivation or urgency to do something different.

The best stories create that sense of urgency, which in turn ignites positive emotion, and is the antidote for the questions, fears, and anxieties that translate into negative behaviors.

It's not uncommon for the importance of *emotion-driven* communication to be brushed aside by leaders in favor of the e-mail newsletter. A colleague was contacted by the VP of human resources of a large shipping company. He said that their company would announce on the following Friday that they were being acquired by another shipping company. "We'd like to talk to you about communicating this to our employees," they requested of our colleague. When he met with the company's leadership two days prior to the announcement, they handed him a two-page memo for his review. That was it – a single two-page memo to address all the anxieties, fears, questions, and concerns about what the acquisition was about and what it meant to the people in the company.

"How have we become so callused?" was his question . . . and an extremely important one. Most leaders can understand the importance of communication, but very few *really* see it through well enough to move their business results forward.

"Seeing it through" means creating a story and engaging people in many ways over a period of time. In this story, a leader must answer questions people *want to know* during change: "Why are we doing this?" "What happens if we don't?" You not only win at the ROI game, but you win people's hearts. This is a lot harder to do than writing an email or composing a letter, but far more predictive of commitment and, therefore, success.

Vision Is the Constant

It's not enough to tell the story once. Amidst the rapid-fire shifts, information overload, and external pressures most organizations are facing, human beings increasingly need to be reminded: "What's the same?" " What's *not* changing?"

The need for routine, constancy, and consistency amidst change is not an accidental wish.

In the popular sci-fi television series *Lost*, Desmond was a character caught between two worlds: His consciousness alternated between two periods of time about eight years apart. He eventually became unable to distinguish between the past, present and future, which led to great disorientation and intense physical symptoms. He was instructed that he must choose a "constant" – someone in both time periods whom he cared about and could recognize. Without a constant, his symptoms would worsen, eventually causing brain aneurysm and death.

His "constant" choice was Penny – the great love of his life. Whenever his disorientation intensified, he *must* find a way to call Penny (given he was stranded on a deserted island, no small feat!).

In these chaotic times, people often feel they are being pulled in several directions at once, with no unifying thread of constancy. In the midst of unprecedented overload, continuous change, and lack of "steady state" in business, people are struggling to find their constant -- a continuous thread that knits together the past, present, and future on initiatives and projects. What keeps everyone centered, focused, and clear-headed? If you have ever tried to balance on one leg, you understand the point of keeping your focus on an unchanging, fixed point. During change, the leader's purpose, vision and values are that focal point. Staring at the horizon – taking your attention OFF the waves or the tipping of the boat – keeps you from becoming disoriented and seasick.

Michael's Story

To illustrate the power of a constant, we share the story of Michael, whose team we helped to develop a strategic plan. Michael leads a bio-energy research institute at a national laboratory. His organization has been inundated with growth and change in the past two years. In the rapidly changing field of renewable energy, the variables, unknowns, and change are at a peak level. Scientists who have spent 30 years in a laboratory quietly doing research are suddenly on the world stage, with significant demands on their time and urgency. This has thrown Michael's entire institute out of its comfort zone. Knowing what to respond to, what to ignore, and how to speed up without losing its identity has been a very challenging task.

Michael expressed what vision means to him in this circumstance: "Our strategic plan was conceived from the beginning as an implementation plan." Leaders have to have great vision, but they also have to be clear and patient, to allow time for the vision to grow and evolve. In my last corporate job, they changed the business plan every 6 months. It gave no time for the organization to "catch up" with the vision. It felt like being on a cruise liner where the leaders were constantly yanking the helm to the right, then to the left, and expecting people would not get seasick. I'm a firm believer in change – but when you introduce it at too rapid a rate, you don't give people time to adapt.

When you are surrounded by anxiety and constant demands to do more, faster, a strong leader has to ignore some of that in order to deflect people who are trying to make things happen faster and faster. While we can't afford to work in glacial time frames, we have to decide what must not change; to be conscious about what we must hold steady to in the face of rapid, continuous growth and change.

You have to hold true to your own belief that change cannot sustain as fast as people are demanding it, so the changes can filter effectively into the culture and integrate with the ongoing work that must be done."

Vision is the critical "constant." Leaders need to tell one story *more* often during increased change. Regular, steady, unchanging communication about the *one thing* that everyone cares about and has an emotional connection to is an organizational version of a constant – a "call to Penny." When working with an executive team, we often coach them to build a list of common phrases that they all use to tell their vision story. This is a simple way to give the organization a feeling that they are aligned. In times when you are uncertain, off-course, disoriented, or beaten down, re-connecting to your emotional constant – the story – is essential. It's about remembering your passion. Today's leaders must see themselves as the organization's anchor to the "constant" – stoking the fiery passion of vision – for the dozens, hundreds, or thousands of people who are seeking more from their daily commitment than a paycheck.

In Chapter 6, we have more to say about this subject, especially for leaders who think they communicate enough.

Remember our client, Bill, from our Introduction: the leader whom Lisa caught off guard by asking him about the CEO's vision for change? We discovered an interesting truth about Bill throughout the course of our work together: Bill HAD that big vision for change. He was crystal clear about where the organization needed to go next. He was not the CEO (nor did he report to the C-level), but Bill is one of those rare leaders who never considered his positioning inside the company a limitation. He 100% believed he was empowered to make real, meaningful change happen within his domain, and that his vision for change would be a stepping stone to restoring the organization to its former glory.

The power of Bill's story was twofold: (1) It was very simple: "We *can* change . . . we *must* try . . . yes it will be hard. We are not going to boil the ocean or set about to 'fix a broken culture' – we are going to fix what we can, and by doing so, prove to ourselves that we are relevant and capable of greatness." (2) In almost every meeting we attended where Bill was present, once the goals were clearly established, he would repeat almost these exact words: "We can change . . . we must try . . . and sometimes it will be hard." (Often followed by a simple question: "How can I help?") A brilliantly simple message that let people know he was committed, that he expected *them* to be committed, and that he knew it would be hard. There was more to what he said, but this core essence of his message signaled to his people the bar had been raised; he had their back; and he was not going to accept failure as an option.

For a quick temperature check of the heat of your fire, pay attention around you. If you are communicating a powerful story, people will be visibly excited, clear and inspired by the vision, and you will see a smooth pathway to getting your projects on time and on budget.

Illustrating the Power of Storytelling

We illustrate this concept of vision and storytelling, through three examples of powerful leadership stories.

Story One: "Tell Them The Story"

"**W**hat's the story Tom? Tell me the story, Tom. I want to know the story."

Tom Downs had been the chairman and CEO of Amtrak for only a few weeks in 1993, during which he primarily spent his time listening to Amtrak employees and customers. "Our people want to know the story. They want to know what's going on. They don't want anything mysterious – just the straight stuff, the truth.

"So we need to be able to tell our story, an honest, credible story that our management team can communicate throughout the corporation. It's something we've got to talk and walk," Downs said. During the next few weeks, Downs created what he referred to as "The Amtrak Story," literally a story about Amtrak's past, present and future.

After assembling 115 of his top managers for a conference for the first time in his tenure, he began:

If you go away remembering absolutely nothing else about this meeting, I want you to remember one thing: always tell the truth. Tell the truth to each other, to our employees, to our customers, to our communities, and to the political and regulatory bodies that we associate with. Always tell the truth.

This is the story of a railroad that must become obsessed with serving its customers or it will go the way of drive-in theaters, full-service gas stations, and downtown shopping.

Amtrak was born old. It opened for business in 1971 with 450 worn-out locomotives, 40-year-old steam-heated passenger cars, an antiquated reservation system, and several inefficient maintenance facilities owned by other railroads.

There have been many improvements over the years. But the railroad never caught up. Since its birth, Amtrak's nearly 25,000 hardworking, railroad-loving employees fought and cursed old systems, processes, and equipment in order to do their jobs. It's a wonder they did as well as they did.

But that was then. This is now.

Today the railroad is in trouble – big, deep trouble.

Equipment is still old and in disrepair. In an effort to live within our budgets, we've repaired old equipment at the expense of buying new equipment.

We've had bad luck. Weather and accidents caused by factors out of our control have been expensive and placed a cloud over the railroad.

Customer expectations are accelerating as airlines work hard to meet customer needs for high quality, service and value.

A constant struggle to reduce costs has reduced service.

An antiquated organizational structure and inadequate resources continue to make it difficult for our 25,000 employees to serve their customers. People can endure only so much before they lose the spirit and enthusiasm that's necessary to win in today's environment.

Customers feel it. They're looking to other forms of transportation, many who've undergone the kinds of changes we must undergo.

Already this year we are $109 million behind our original forecast. This is the equivalent of 54 new low-level cars, 36 locomotives, salaries for 2,400 customer service employees for a year, or huge improvements in our Sunnyside, Beach Grove, or Wilmington facilities. We're in a deep hole. We're in deep trouble. For Amtrak to survive, we must fundamentally change the organization. Fundamental does not mean tweak here, fine tune there. It does not mean do what we've always done, but better.

Amtrak must be reinvented. It must be reinvented in the form of a modern, customer-obsessed, high-performing organization.

It must begin with an intense and simultaneous focus on the two most important groups of people in Amtrak's world – our customers and our employees.

We must create a partnership between our customers, who demand quality, service, and value, and our employees, who get up every day wanting to do what's right by the customer. This kind of partnership will create a financially strong business. A financially strong business will be very attractive to our other business partners at the federal, state and local levels.

We have already begun to reinvent Amtrak. Here's what we're doing (lists a dozen or so initiatives that are underway, making the point that everyone has the responsibility to reinvent Amtrak).

What does reinventing Amtrak mean?

For leaders throughout Amtrak it means communicating with everything they say and do that we have no choice but to create a fundamentally different railroad – a railroad that is dramatically tilted toward the customer. Amtrak leaders must be in charge of dramatically improving the system, removing system defects that cause dissatisfied customers. Our leaders must look for every opportunity to make sure that our employees have the resources – including money, tools, and information – needed to take care of the customers.

For all our employees, it means viewing the customer as your only boss. Our employees have a responsibility to identify areas for improvement and then help improve them. They need to seek the skills, information, and tools they need to improve quality, service and value.

Reinventing Amtrak will mean assuming different roles and responsibilities. It will mean trying new things on behalf of the customer.

Reinventing Amtrak also means a new relationship between the organization and our employees. Amtrak was born out of a paternalistic and authoritarian environment. The company knew what was best for its employees. If the employees did as they were told, the organization would take care of them – provide regular pay increases and some measure of job security. The paternalistic relationship may have worked well in the past. It doesn't today. World-class performance around quality, service, costs, speed and innovation doesn't come from controlled, protected people who are taken care of. It comes from informed, engaged business people who are held accountable for the organization's success. That's the Amtrak we must create.

Many people will find the process of reinventing Amtrak to be an exciting and rewarding one. Some will be uncomfortable in the new environment. They may find comfort going elsewhere. We thank them for their contributions and recognize them as important Amtrak alumni.

We are America's railroad. We cannot continue to survive if we don't reinvent Amtrak. We can become the world's best passenger railroad.

It will take time, down-in-the-trenches hard work, and an unwavering focus on our customers and our employees. Getting there will be at once exciting and painful, exhilarating and frustrating. But when we get there, it will have been worth the ride.

When he finished, Amtrak's managers gave him a standing ovation. He'd said things they all knew and felt, but that nobody had said until Downs said them.

"Tell the story again and again," Downs urged his managers. "And just when you think you've told it enough times, tell it one more time."

Throughout the Tom Downs years at Amtrak, there were two communication principles at work: (1) Always tell the story; and (2) Always tell the truth. By the time he left in 1997, the Board of directors commended Downs for "helping Amtrak become more business and customer oriented; obtaining outstanding gains in revenues and ridership during his tenure; and for leading the recent fight for a S2.3 billion dedicated capital improvements fund for Amtrak." [11]

Story Two: "Are We Going to Empty the Buckets or Fix the Roof?"

At one of the largest pharmaceutical companies in the U.S., our client had just been put in charge of quality. That happened when the FDA issued a Consent Decree on this company. A Consent Decree means that the company violated government mandated "Good Manufacturing Practices" for so long that the FDA issued a court order to impose massive fines if the company did not fix the problems post haste.

Our client had taken a job with this company with the hope of having a quiet time running part of their manufacturing operation, having just saved another huge pharmaceutical from a near-miss Consent Decree. When his new company asked the FDA how they could possibly correct the many violations of law that they had been charged with, the FDA agent said: "Hire the best quality guy we know. And, he already works for you."

With thousands of employees spread over manufacturing sites on four continents, this was a daunting task. Especially given how far their standards had sunk under previous leadership (lack of leadership). As our client became educated about the extent of the problem, he saw an example of the problem and turned it into a rallying cry for the entire effort. While visiting with the Quality Group at a plant in Puerto Rico, he discovered that for several years, there had been a leak in the roof of one of the buildings that made a sophisticated and sensitive biological product. The solution to the leak had been to place a bucket under the leak and empty it whenever it was full of rainwater (which in Puerto Rico was frequently). As he traveled the globe talking about how to avoid the Consent Decree, he told the story of the bucket and the rain, and concluded with the question: "Are we going to empty the bucket or fix the roof?"

This simple statement *became* the vision.

Story Three: "A Coffee Dream "

As I (Lisa) pulled up to the drive-through for my wet skinny cappuccino with a shot of pumpkin spice, I was handed a piece of white paper with a bold title at the top: "The Starbucks Coffee New World Record for the fastest, friendliest drive-through is about to be set at Wadsworth & Bowles." It went on to describe the specific ways customers could help that Starbucks store win their challenge ("What you can do to help us succeed"). Seconds later, the guy at the window handed me my drink and asked, "Does that feel like the right weight to you?" (a sign of someone who's trying to please their customer).

Fast-forward to a week after the deadline. This time I enter the store seeking research with my caffeine. Here's how it went:

I ask the guy behind the counter "Did you win?"

"Oh yeah, we totally set the new world record."

"How did that feel?"

"AWESOME. We were so energized, it really pulled our team together, got everyone involved, you know? We had a great time."

"Did you get any financial incentive for it?"

"Uh, no. It was just a lot of fun. We were looking to lower our drive-through speed anyway, and so we came up with this as a fun way to make it happen. There were a couple of guys who just OWNED it, really made it fun, made it happen and it caught on – everyone was pulling for it."

A Final Note for Our Left-Brain Friends

A vision can be fun and energizing, catalyze teamwork, align people to a cause, AND improve the business.

And, it's important to back it up with facts and analysis. Leading is a "whole-brain" activity – not just drawing from the creative side of the brain.

Great storytelling is inspiring; at the same time, a clear objective holds people's focus and attention in a single-pointed fashion. Sports are a good example – there's no ambiguity about who won the game when the time is up. This is the level of clarity people need and want in a goal.

In order to do that, your story should address both sides of human psychology — the need for logic and the need for emotional connection.

The end result? More people carrying your torch.

SUMMARY
Nature's Truth #2:

In nature, movement typically follows the path of least resistance.

In business, movement forward is catalyzed by shared vision:

It is the fire of motivation.

1. **For maximum motivation, use language that helps people commit toward something they want, and away from something they can see should be avoided.**

2. **Build a story to draw out emotion through logic.**

3. **Tell your story often and in many ways: use it as a constant during change.**

Making It Work! Small Changes for Developing a Story of Vision

We know business is not a bedtime ritual of fairy tales. It's about balancing analysis, logic, reason, AND building a good story that draws on people's emotions and makes them want to commit. Tom Down's Amtrak story did a great job of blending both.

Building a good story takes some thought and time. (Then again, so does building 450 PowerPoint slides analyzing the facts and figures.)

The criteria for a powerful story include:

1) Creates pain AND inspires – i.e., builds a maximum motivational state of urgency

2) Draws upon metaphor, which engages people's emotion ("My love is like a rose." "Our competitive landscape has moved from baseball to tennis.")

3) Is easy to identify with – aligns with our experience of the world
(Life is like a box of chocolates – you never know what you're going to get." "Amtrak was born old.")

4) Speaks to our highest aspirations
(Missions that emphasize creativity, service, or solving a grand problem sustain more energy and commitment than those which call upon reduction (cost-cutting), money, or competition. "Are we going to empty the buckets or fix the roof?")

5) Tells us what to DO to implement our strategy
"Let's set the new world record for the fastest Starbucks drive-through service.")

6) Creates a connection with the storyteller and tells the truth – the "believability" factor (If you don't believe it, neither will anyone else.)

One final cautionary note: Vision is not a substitute for action. Too many leaders spend too much time wordsmithing the vision.

Get your story focused and start telling it – as a catalyst for action, not a substitute.

Chapter 3: TRUST
Trust Is Like the Sun

In Chapter 3, we explore the importance of trust – and its role in a healthy culture. Like the sun, trust is the essential life energy for all growth. The passionate vision leaders carry must be communicated in a way that builds trust that the leaders know where we are headed and can take us there.

Trust Is Like the Sun

Nature's Truth #3:

In nature, the sun is the source of all life.

In business, trust is the essential energy in which lasting change occurs, continuously.

"You must trust and believe in people or life becomes impossible."

— Anton Chekhov, Russian author and playwright

Remember the last time you watched a sunrise or sunset and became awe-inspired? That beauty is never tarnished with the question: "I wonder if the Sun will rise again tomorrow?" We always trust that it will, providing the right amount of light and heat for eternity (or another 5 billion years or so).

Here on Earth, the Sun is the ultimate power source: self-sustaining and infinite in its capacity to create growth.

For leaders, trust is the human equivalent of the Sun. The ability to radiate trust throughout your team and business in a way that is as reliable as the Sun is the source of all growth – whether growth in revenue, in customer satisfaction scores, or in adoption of your new technology. Without trust, your plans, initiatives and projects will *never* put down sustainable roots to thrive and grow over time.

Unfortunately, trust has been eroded substantially in today's businesses, families, and society at large.

Given trust is the first stage an infant must pass through to develop into a healthy person (from 0 to 18 months according to Erik Erikson's psychosocial development theory)[12] why would it be any different for an organization – which is simply a collection of people? Leaders who understand this are always mindful of whether their actions build trust – or erode it.

In our technology-driven business world, we often inadvertently eliminate the real source of power in our organizations: "The human factor" is seen as an "extra" or "nice-to have," rather than something to actively manage and pay attention to. This is like placing a plant in a dark cave away from the Sun and hoping it will grow simply by telling it you want it to grow. You don't get growth by focusing on growth. You get growth by focusing on the elements that *produce* growth. The sunlight in business is an environment in which teams can trust their leader and each other.

The Trust Gap

Employees Assume Their Company Will . . .	Leaders . . .
Empower me . . . reward me . . . but won't micro-manage me.	Assume employees are grown-ups and can take initiative to solve problems.
Take care of the details.	Don't have time to baby-sit projects.
Invest in my career.	Often eliminate programs that develop employees because they're plagued by tight margins.
Provide ALL the resources needed to ensure projects are on-time and on-budget.	Know that throwing more money at the problem won't fix it.
Teach me how to catch on to the hidden nuances of communication and decision-making.	Assume effective communication is happening below them, and will take care of itself.

Any business outcome you seek – improved productivity, growth in market share or improving work processes – won't take hold or sustain in a void of trust. Leaders must learn to stimulate growth with zealous efforts to cultivate trust through relationship, connection, and meaning. It's not easy in a society where the central measurement of success is money, not relationships – even though studies on what motivates people list money nowhere near the top. (If you're skeptical, take out a piece of paper right now and list the top five values *you* hold near and dear. If money were *really* #1 on that list you wouldn't be reading this.)

Cultivating trust is not optional. It's a crucial element of a leader's job description. Two words tell the story:

Ask Why.

Two words with huge meaning.

"Ask Why" became the symbol of the Enron meltdown.

What's most concerning about Enron is that in spite of the scale of that lesson, it's still happening eight years later. As of the writing of this book, Goldman Sachs was charged with fraud by the U.S. Securities and Exchange Commission for marketing a debt product tied to subprime mortgages designed to fail.[13] The lawsuit is the biggest crisis in years for Goldman after emerging from the global financial crisis in 2007-08 as Wall Street's most influential bank. (It remains to be seen if Goldman Sachs is simply a poster child for the targeted reform or truly a culpable player in this house of cards.) Either way, the central message is this: People don't know who or what they can trust.

What Does Trust Mean for Leaders Today?

First, in the past, leaders were trusted by virtue of their position. That was shattered by Enron, and reinforced years later by a steady stream of similar meltdowns. Leaders cannot assume "automatic trust." They must earn it.

Second, in an environment of constant change, people's fears are "up." Trust is the anchor they can return to. "What's going to happen next?" "What can I count on?" "Will I have a job?" When the world no longer operates by the simple rules of the past, leaders need to *over*-compensate through steady, consistent efforts to keep their word and stay committed to their vision.

Third, actively building environments in which trust flourishes is the foundation of creativity. People don't take risks in environments where trust is low and fear is high. A recession economy provides a good opportunity to prune excess and cost from systems, renew your business model, and develop people. Businesses that are creative can define new ways to survive and thrive with fewer resources.

On the flip side is the equation of how leaders trust their people. In Karen Stephenson's pioneering work on organizational change outlined in her article *The Quantum Theory of Trust*,[14] she contends: "The association between trust and learning is a vast, untapped source of organizational power. People have at their fingertips tremendous amounts of knowledge that aren't captured in computer systems or on paper. Trust is the utility through which this knowledge flows. Her premise (based on social research) is that high trust societies have enormous competitive advantage in a global economy, because their transactional costs are lower. We see this in action in communities where a handshake is still a binding contract in business – and the commensurate legal fees are much lower. As pointed out in the Introduction of our book, American companies spend three times more on litigation than on research.

Dutch traffic engineer Hans Monderman writes: "The greater the number of prescriptions, the more people's sense of personal responsibility dwindles." (In his blunter version: "When you treat people like idiots, they'll behave like idiots.") If people are bound by too many rules, they become less mindful of their impact on others and more fearful. Significant creativity and intelligence is repressed or unavailable in cultures in which punitive retaliation and fear are dominant.

A client in a recent training program said it well: "You can't legislate respect. My experience is that it usually comes from the top down, with people walking their walk and talking their talk. There's nothing like others seeing a manager support someone for the decision that they've made and having that person know that they will be backed. True empowerment is so strong . . . not only in terms of people taking ownership of their decisions, but also for the whole company." Too often, we attempt to bypass the essential energy source of trust and grow "plant factories" that never see sunlight. The new wave of employee engagement programs is a good example. Surveys on workplace engagement, engagement workshops and diversity training are initiated from the top or delegated to HR, but leaders – overworked and overwhelmed – don't socialize these ideas via meaningful dialogue with the people who will implement them. Too much is lost in translation; and too little real change sticks as a result. The evidence? Gallup's statistics on workplace engagement haven't changed in several years: two out of three employees AND managers are either actively disengaged (acting out their unhappiness) or not engaged (checked out).

Gerry has known and worked with Rebecca for years, manager of a customer service department in a major healthcare insurance company. Rebecca is not a whiner, nor does she lack in personal responsibility. In fact, she uses many of the *Small Change* principles in her efforts to protect her people and customers from what she feels is a dysfunctional and toxic organization: one that is in desperate need of true leadership and change, but is approaching it in all the wrong ways. After nearly 25 years of service, she is sad that the organization's shining star of greatness and competence has fallen so far.

Rebecca's story:

O ur organization is a poster child for "Flavor of the Month." Over the past 15+ years, we have been through continuous cycles of change processes, or at least attempts at change. Every 18 months to two years, like clockwork, leadership begins a new one. There are two problems with these programs, which always follow the same pattern:

First, the leaders kick off the program. Then, within a few weeks, they quickly seem to lose interest – it's like "we've done our part, now go make it happen." Or perhaps they feel that it is not them that needs to change, but rather everyone else. There is very little follow through, and even less communication about much of anything related to the program: evidence it's succeeding, positive reinforcement, or linkage to our strategy and goals.

The people in the organization make some effort to "get on board," but before we can find our footing with one set of new approaches and skills, the leaders are onto a new one.

The second and bigger problem is that leadership behavior is often completely incongruent with the very programs they initiate. For instance, the latest program has "personal accountability" as a key message. Yet, our leadership consistently blames others when things don't go well. I have never seen a senior leader in our organization publicly admit an error. People are said to be empowered and are asked to contribute ideas to help us grow. However, when someone makes a decision that doesn't go well, they are punished. Offering any suggestion, even if it is constructive, usually results in criticism or punishment. It's gotten to the point where even our strongest contributors don't feel safe speaking up.

To complicate matters, we're downsizing because of financial pressures. That's been handled so poorly that it has created an environment of fear. Like many organizations, one of the programs we did was the Q-12 by Gallup. It was supposed to be about improving employee satisfaction and engagement. When a program is intended to support people feeling more engaged and satisfied at work, it raises people's hopes and expectations. What happened instead is the entire process highlighted in painful full color that our organization doesn't care about our satisfaction any more. We'd have been better off not doing anything! Leaders say they want improvement and ideas, but the real message is their behavior: if you are not a person who "puts a smile on and doesn't make waves," you'll be fired. In these difficult financial times, having a job is about survival, and losing one can feel like a death sentence.

Whenever someone is walked out of the building, gossip begins about why they were let go. It is usually assumed they were not compliant enough. We've learned to keep our mouths shut, and the terms "empowerment" and "engagement" are a meaningless, cruel joke.

An additional cause of the morale issue is that communication has been so poor. When a major change is coming, we get an email. It's always issued around 4:00 on a Friday afternoon. I wonder if they think we'll forget over the weekend? Or, if they think by delivering the news on Friday, when Monday morning comes everything will start fresh, like it never happened? I would say this has undermined trust, but it's hard to go below zero.

All of these programs were supposed to change our culture. And it has succeeded! We now have a culture of fear and complete disengagement.

Unfortunately, Rebecca's story is all too common in today's corporate environments. Even worse, executives are often completely unaware of the fact their employees and managers feel this way. Executives may not be fully at fault for this situation, but they *are* responsible for the solution. What is that solution?

We say this: Drop the programs and start getting REAL about what actually builds trust. Trust is created through a consistent assumption of positive intent and curiosity about the other person's point of view. It is built on attention to relationship, interaction and conversation. It requires conscious attention to aligning your thoughts, your words and your deeds. No change programs, surveys, training or compensation plans can substitute for trust, which is built on character, keeping your word and demonstrating good decisions. It's eroded by a perception of haphazard, desperate efforts to chase profits, and not being connected to shared purpose and vision.

If you want more engagement – you must see it as the END RESULT of strong trust, not the SOURCE. Leaders with rampant lack of trust around their organization need to muster the courage to look in the mirror at the *real* messages they are sending through their behavior, not the words from their lips.

There's no shortcut and there's no substitute for a truly trusting environment, earned by becoming worthy of people's trust.

Trust and Change Are a Group-Thing

What are the best ways to build trust if you're leading change? In today's complex organizations it is more than ensuring you are *personally* trustworthy.

Remember our friends Bill and Dan from the Introduction? Trust was a fragile alliance across their company. When Bill took over the technology organization in November of 2009, its reputation across the company was "always late, always over-budget." The business unit leader (let's call him Charles) and the product delivery executive (Dan) needed Bill's technology to be "on time and on budget" to ensure the growth of a $4 billion market play. They had been trying to get a software platform from Bill's predecessor for four years. The result? He is still not able to competitively deliver products in a timely fashion in his market due to a continuous stream of development delays. In two years, his R&D costs grew by $16M, while all other business units' costs went down. Charles' trust in the success of this initiative – and the path Bill was recommending – was ROCK BOTTOM. While Dan had concerns, he had chosen to put them aside and believe in Bill's leadership.

Over the next several months, our leaders from the technology company Bill, Dan and Charles engaged in a regular series of heated, hard-hitting, honest conversations. Charles' trust grew in Bill and Dan as leaders, but he remained untrusting of the *process*. This leaked out in how he communicated and where he chose to be visible. This "trust" issue was debilitating to the team's work, and had to be addressed. Bill and Dan directly discussed this situation with Charles, and contracted for a different kind of trust: the trust that we (Bill and Dan) will do whatever we can to make this work. Dan told Charles: "I need you to trust our *commitment*. Of course we can fail. But we don't consider failure an option. We are staying in constant dialogue with you so you know what measures and steps we are taking to keep the promise and ensure we *don't* fail. Can you trust *that*?" This created a significant breakthrough in Charles' trust – and released a lot of energy downstream.

By the way, we are not suggesting that Charles' mistrust was misplaced – anyone in his shoes would be wary after four years of empty promises that didn't deliver.

But in today's complex matrix organizations, leaders owe it to their teams and organizations to dig beneath the surface with *each other* and explore how they can visibly show an aligned, supportive front to their organizations. Otherwise, lack of trust in each other trickles and cascades throughout the entire team and organization. This lack of alignment manifests as constant second-guessing and decision paralysis. Ironically, lack of willingness to trust each other at the top – and agree to principles that build trust in each other – backfires, creating the exact opposite of the speed leaders need. When people don't see leaders trust — productivity always suffers.

Every case of underperformance in a specific department or area of a business we have diagnosed can be traced to a lack of alignment and trust in leaders. In fact, the trust problem typically escalates at least 2-3 levels higher than where the problem exists.

Leaders must ask themselves at every turn: "Does what I am doing right now build or erode the "trust capital" in my organization or team?" Trust is what converts energy to commitment, the stored energy that drives productive action. This productivity cycle is the only way innovation and growth happen – like a social photosynthesis, trust converts energy from the leaders into aligned action. It's catching!

The Sun is so powerful that even the very small
amount that falls on Earth sustains all life (only 0.00000002% of
the total Sun's energy reaches the Earth.)

In his book "Viral Change",[15] Leandro Herrero writes: "75% of the
work conversations that drive problem solving, knowledge transfer
and new ideas occur in the invisible, informal networks between
people in organizations."

What are people saying about your leadership in those conversations?

Even a small amount of work to build trust in your organization can
make a significant difference – it all goes back to your intention.

Four Pillars of Trust

There is a process and a structure to building stronger trust. Let's explore the four Pillars of Trust that transform energy into growth in your team or organization.

1. Alignment & Positive Intent: Hard-Wired for Likeness

2. Candor: The Lost Art of Truth-Telling

3. Transparency: It's Time Has Come

4. Empowerment: It's Not a Group Activity.

The 1st Pillar: Alignment: Hard-Wired for Likeness

The latest research on how the brain works (the field of neuroscience) provides profound insights about how people really think, act and function in relationships.

Much of what we *thought* to be true about human motivation is proving to be both incomplete and wrong. For example, Taylorism beliefs that "men work harder when offered financial incentives" and "men don't want to think" have been completely debunked in modern psychology. Science now provides the proof: Through comprehensive research in neuroscience, we are learning exactly what is taking place in the brain during communication and relationship-building. From this, we can learn to be more purposeful and conscious about how we build connections with people. You can create major breakthroughs in growth and innovation by putting this simple notion into practice.

One of these breakthroughs is the simple truth that human beings are "hard-wired" for empathy, connection and cooperation (to seek "like" in one another AND to support their tribe). No surprise here. What *is* surprising is that the business world is set up to cultivate and reward the opposite: individualism and competition *within the tribe*. The discovery of "mirror neurons," nerve cells discovered by Italian neuroscientist Giacomo Rizzolatti, were found by accident while working with monkeys. The *same* neuron fires in the monkey's brain when he raises his arm as when he simply observed the action of a human raising an arm.

Mirror neurons are what Daniel Goleman calls "neural Wi-Fi" in his book *Social Intelligence*. Deeper research shows that spindle cells in our brains are part of a system that enables us to detect another person's feelings as if they are our own – so when we are really tuned in, we aren't kidding when we say, "I feel your pain." There is a third type of neuron called "oscillators" that coordinate how people respond to each other with movement. You can see oscillators in action when you watch two friends embrace; their movements are a dance, one body responding to the other seamlessly. Collectively, these three sets of neurons work together and are referred to by behavioral scientists as our social guidance system.

Traditional cultures intuitively understood these characteristics before the research proved it. Every culture understands: "You can't understand someone unless you walk a mile in her shoes." This is a powerful metaphor for what the best leaders do to build trust. In business, "feeling your pain" looks like "I know it's been frustrating that we can't share the details of our plans, but here's what we do know." Or, "I am sorry there is so much uncertainty about the job situation in our business. Please know that for us as leaders, cutting jobs is a last resort – we'll take every step possible to avoid it." Or, "We are wondering what we can do to help answer questions, and understand that in many cases WE don't know the answers, but we'll be available to answer what we can." Transparency is the name of the game today.

In our coaching work, teaching leaders to align more with the point of view of their stakeholders is probably one of the top three skills we focus on. It's like health – you cannot have "too much alignment." (Aligning is NOT buying their story or giving them anything they want – it's just acknowledging what's true for them. This is 100% based on the assumption of positive intention – that the other person is doing the best they can do, and is not seeking to be deceptive or hide the truth. (Even if they are, it's almost never useful to assume it in your communications.)

When you're in disagreement or not comfortable with what is happening in communication, find a way to make a statement that assumes you can find a middle ground, versus one that assumes the other person is wrong and you are right. "I think you are off-track here" is based on a very different assumption than, "I think we are not fully aligned about what we each expect." If you watch the best relationship-builders you can observe that they systematically *align* with elements of the person or people they are talking to, and usually assume positive intent. This is conveyed through what they say, but more importantly, through their nonverbal behavior.

This is what helps people connect and feel that they are alike. And when people feel alike, i.e., they feel part of the same tribe, this becomes a foundational building block of long-term trust.

Every leader's job is to lead people toward a desired vision or direction. The fastest way to get someone to follow is to *first* align with some aspect of where they are today; *then* lead. Less skilled leaders will try to lead before aligning – to insert their point of view and rationale into the situation and then try to convince people why it's right. That doesn't work nearly as well, and it doesn't build relationship in which collaborative leadership can flourish. It reinforces the command-and-control hierarchy.

In the business world today, people are often assigned bosses, alliances or roles on teams with people they have never met. Meetings are increasingly virtual, with people at their desks versus in a room together. In this situation, "mirror neurons" – the building block that establishes a trust foundation – are *absent*. When sensory-based social signals are missing, people often interpret leaders' or teammates' actions they don't agree with as "that person cannot be trusted."

Unfortunately, as we will learn in Chapter 8, this interpretation is mostly unconscious and out of people's awareness. Misinterpretation is causing rampant "e-flail," long email chains defending territory, decisions and actions without picking up the phone and talking. One innocent sentence in an email can become a trigger: "If you are not able to meet this deadline I will find someone else who can" may be read as inflammatory, when the sender meant it as a straightforward commentary about fulfilling the deadline. If your knowledge of this person is limited or missing, you have just thrown the first dart without even realizing it. As a result of the "virtual world" we work in, we observe leaders spending WAY too much time sorting out e-flail trails and composing sentences carefully to avoid misinterpretation.

Trust can be grown from one powerful seed called "assume positive intent" – and the willingness to pick up the phone more often!

The Trust Formula

The Untrained Manager:
Lead ⇨ *Before* You Align
(too often, no aligning at all!)

The Effective Leader:
Align ⇨ *Then* Lead
(*after* you have established rapport)

Aligning with someone is only one side of the equation. Leaders' emotions and actions prompt others to mirror back their feelings and actions. (Research shows that nonverbal expressions of body language carry much of the vast majority of meaning in communication. Up to 93% of the meaning is interpreted not by the words, but by body language, tone of voice, etc. It's not what you say, it's how you say it!)

As "people-geeks" we learned something fascinating in the research for this book: It turns out that mirror neurons have specialist positions. There's a whole category whose job it is to detect smiles and laughter in others. A boss who is cold, self-controlled and humorless rarely fires off "smile neurons" in team members. In contrast, a boss who laughs and sets an easygoing tone that puts people at ease will see those neurons at work in a way that triggers laughter, which in turn bonds the team more strongly. And a bonded group performs well. Top-performing leaders elicited laughter from subordinates an average of three times as often as mid-performing leaders.

As Daniel Goleman puts it: "Laughter is serious business."

We have had the good fortune to work with several leaders who sought coaching to develop "smile neurons" (not always just smiles but positive, fun energy) which spread positive emotions in addition to smiles. During a particularly challenging time in his division, a client who was the SVP of manufacturing was practicing his weekly walking tour of the plant. We could practically see him activate the mirror neurons, spindle cells and oscillators in all the people he encountered. He smiled radiantly at the first machine operator he saw, commenting on a recent accomplishment that caught his attention. He shook hands with a janitor, pausing to make a personal comment and pat him on the back. Moving on, he spotted someone from another department and gave her a hug, asking her if she was "working across boundaries" and then thanking her when she told him what she was doing. In each case, he made eye contact, matched his body language to theirs, and found a way to say "thanks" to each person for their contribution. We watched each person respond in kind, giving him back almost exactly what he offered. The boost in morale was palpable in the wake of his walking around.

We are not advocating Pollyanna behavior or burying the truth – Enron taught us what happens when leaders do that. This advice is about focusing people's attention on what IS positive and building relationships and connection.

The problem – which in many ways states the obvious – is that the business and organizational world has built structures and rituals that train us to act *against* our natural inclinations much of the time. Performance management systems are set up to create a power mismatch in relationships. Strategic planning exercises rarely involve teams who implement – the brains (leaders) are disconnected from the body (the front line employees). Bonuses are often based on results that pit departments against one another for scarce resources.

As Dan, Bill and Charles showed us, alignment is not an easy or natural activity in business.

Mark Durliat took a different approach to aligning his team. When Mark discovered Grace Bay Club in the Caribbean area of Turks/Caicos, it looked like the perfect investment. He bought the property in 2001 with plans to turn it into a premier resort. The next day, his newly acquired staff, in its entirety, went on strike. "They all expected to be fired" he recalls, and felt they were entitled to severance." Durliat walked into a meeting of angry workers and spent hours listening patiently to their complaints. After they had cooled down, he explained his intentions were to build a Caribbean hotel with Caribbean employees – whatever that took. The next day, they were back at work.

This was only the beginning – the employees in this resort were friendly and caring, but had never been trained on how to cater to a well-heeled clientele. He describes the change began with listening: "Here, it's all about who you are and how you're treated." For three months, all he did was develop relationships, not changing anything. Instead, he "shook hands, walked around and learned how things worked." He often worked side by side with the employees. That earned him the right to start making improvements – which took almost two years of his investment to take hold. But today the resort generates $50 million in revenues and attracts A-list clients. Due to Durliat's education, employees understand the value of the improvements he made. "We have to focus on getting better because of the competition out there."

The good news: We are wired to connect. Every interaction with every person in your organization will build more trust if you adopt a posture of alignment *first* – before you make demands.

The 2nd Pillar: Candor – The Lost Art of Truth-Telling

The second pillar of trust is Candor. This is about learning to tell the truth – even (and especially) when it's uncomfortable.

There is no substitute for honest communication and keeping your word. Listen first, then speak simply, with candor. If you know you cannot keep an agreement – even as simple as a project or task deadline – say so. If you break an agreement, apologize. If you don't know what's going on, say what you do know. The bottom line is, don't hide bad news – people will make up stories far worse than anything you could say. You gain a lot of respect by telling people what you DO know. Show up, be humble, and say *something*.

For some reason, we find that executives in particular have a really hard time with this.

Recently, we were having lunch with a leader in a technology company, who was agitated about a recent development at work: "How can I tell my boss he's off track with a new product line? His passion for the project is *personal*: The product uses a hot new technology in which one of his close friends invested heavily, and he's not going to like bad news."

She went on: "What he doesn't know is his pet project is behind two competitors' products that are about to be launched. They have key features ours does not, yet he'd like to position ours with a premium price tag. This will make it almost impossible to gain the leg-up to compete."

This executive — a highly self-confident and respected leader – was literally terrified of offending him by telling the truth. "It's a Career-Limiting Move. People get shot all the time by him."

Our next question to the executive: "What would you do if he were a peer?"

"Take him to lunch and tell him what I know." Within minutes she had stated a clear and simple business case for why the project was at risk. This was based not just on her instinct but on substance; she had the facts and the market intelligence to back it up.

Then we asked, "What would your boss say if he were eavesdropping on this conversation right now?"

Without a second of hesitation she replied: "He'd say, 'Why didn't you tell me sooner?'"

We spent a few minutes talking about *how* to deliver bad news in a way people can hear it. Test it with trusted confidants — yours AND your bosses'. Ask if he wants it before launching. Be sure you have at least two options. Get your facts straight. And, perhaps most important, pick a good time. We then brainstormed a few courses of action she believed would make the project more successful.

This story cuts to the core of authenticity in leadership: One of the toughest tests of authentic leadership is telling someone *else*, especially someone with more authority, a hard truth — with candor. Candor means being frank, open, sincere and free of bias.

Fearlessness and candor are tempered in the fire of practice. Your leadership is never tested with easy decisions. Being prepared to tell a hard truth requires knowing what *you* believe, doing your homework, having diplomacy and being unafraid of the "fallout." You master it in stages. You don't start with the really hard one, but practice it in safe environments first.

If you have a reputation for whining or playing devil's advocate without a solution, you need to develop a style that has a better chance of influencing others. If you aren't practiced at being authentic, start now. When you follow simple practices for being authentic, you earn a reputation for respect. You'll also sleep better at night.

As for our leader? She built her case, told the truth, and was proud of her conviction and clarity. Her boss asked a lot of tough questions, and then thanked her for her input and sent her on her way. Instead of feeling bad that he didn't immediately agree (most executives won't), she walked away satisfied he had the information to make the right decision. The rest was up to him.

And most satisfying, she learned the real career-limiting move is staying silent when the truth needs to be said.

What truth are you hesitating to tell?

The 3rd Pillar: Transparency – Its Time Has Come

There is no time in history where creating more transparency between leaders and their stakeholders seems more relevant.

In Chapter 1, we talked about the largest in-depth study of leadership development ever undertaken, in which the authors asked: "How can people become and remain authentic leaders?" The results were detailed in a February 2007 article in *Harvard Business Review*: "Discovering Your Authentic Leadership," which reported that the key to great leadership is authenticity.

No surprise, but what does it mean?

We all have an immediate "sense" or "gut" feeling about whether we can trust someone or not when we first meet them. Even when someone is abrasive or direct or laughs too much, we may instinctively know they're trustworthy. And someone who is confident and "in possession of themselves" may feel untrustworthy. We have built-in radar-detectors for insincerity, hiding behind a mask, or an agenda of self-interest.

When you exude trust and act trustworthy, you cultivate an aura of trust around you. Remember mirror neurons? They are our "BS Meter" for sincerity (or lack of it). If you see trust problems in your team or organization, look in the mirror. Chances are people don't trust YOU. Get a good coach to help you see and correct your blind spots. And never forget the cardinal rule of communication: Actions speak louder than words.

A second element of transparency is creating an open book management process within your organization or team. The days of the leaders (and maybe the sales department) being the only people who understand the budget and the balance sheet are over. In today's fast-moving, competitive environments, everyone needs to understand how their performance drives the bottom line performance and profitability of the organization.

At one of our clients, an electrical contracting company, we spent hours educating the hourly field workers on the importance of productivity: what it means, what drives it, and how they can impact it. Too often, leaders see their employees as "too dumb to understand" or believe "that's confidential." But in an age of the Internet, where nothing is secret, people expect and want line of sight about how their behavior impacts your goals. Open up.

A third element of transparency is decision making. (We go into detail about the topic of Decision Making in Chapter 4 on the "Structure of Growth.") Engaging people in specific conversations to create shared meaning and understanding is a way to ensure trust becomes the power source in your initiatives and leads to better decisions. Establish "consultative change" as the prevailing wind in your organization. Don't make major changes without first listening to and seeking input from employees. This means having *conversations* about the purpose of change and how it aligns with your values as an organization. This has a practical element as well: The more you talk to the "end users" and "implementers," the faster you will implement change.

The 4th Pillar: Empowerment: It's Not a Group Activity.

In western Massachusetts – and in other locations across the country – there's a growing movement where fresh local food is sold through an honor system of roadside farm stands. The signs are simple: "Fresh Eggs." "Sweet Corn." "Bouquets." You stop, pick up your produce, and leave money in an old coffee can or cigar box. No one supervises the transaction – you are trusted to do right. No surveillance cameras. No Internet monitoring systems. And, while there's the possibility of theft, most people don't steal. In fact, some customers make a point of over-paying, or leaving an I.O.U. note even if it's just for 50 cents. What makes this work? Both parties perceive benefit and are engaged in the transaction.

This is a far cry from the work environments portrayed in the popular TV series, "The Office." Today's employment contracts and work environments often do not benefit both sides nor foster a sense of community. When people feel they're anonymous, being used, or powerless, they look for ways to retaliate or save their discretionary energy and creativity for activities outside work. Trust your people to make more decisions and serve their customers. Educate them about how to do that. When people make mistakes, steer away from blame or punishment – focus on their positive intent and learning. If you have to fire someone who can't do the job, it should never be a surprise.

In the workplace, empowerment is a "one-person-at-a-time" process. You don't empower a "workforce;" you empower individuals who have proven ready. That occurs at the intersection of three main elements:

Empowerment Sweet Spot

In our culture work, we teach that every leader with direct reports should accept the responsibility to actively mentor/develop **at least** two people directly, to increase their ability and responsibility to grow into their next job.

We also teach a series of four powerful *Coaching for Performance* questions leaders can use to build a culture in which feedback is expected, without evoking defensiveness:

1) **What happened? (Just the facts, no blaming or finger-pointing.)**

2) **What have you tried/done to solve this problem?**

3) **What did you learn?**

4) **What will you do differently now . . . or next time?**

Trust is the energy source by which anything grows.

Trust in that and your leadership will change.

SUMMARY
Nature's Truth #3:

In nature, the sun is the source of all life. In business, trust is the essential energy in which lasting change occurs, continuously.

Trust may seem intangible, but leading without it is a root cause of why change initiatives fail. Imagine trying to feed your family by growing plants in your basement (without grow lights). Missing a key ingredient of growth, you are unlikely to produce anything but fungus.

Do more of these 4 "pillar" activities to build trust:

1. **Align before you lead; you are hard-wired to connect and be alike.**

2. **Use candor – there is great power in telling the truth with no spin. (See the last page of this book for how to download a free tool on "Changing Corporate Culture Through Tough Conversations")**

3. **Develop transparency – in today's business climate, people will not trust leaders who hide basic information about the business.**

4. **Empower people who have earned it.**

Making It Work! Small Changes for Building Trust

1) One of the most powerful "small change" practices in this book is simply transformational all by itself. Consider every decision and communication against the following criteria: Will this build trust or erode trust?

2) Keep an "Ask" journal. Note in a week's time how many of your interactions with a subordinate involve YOU asking THEM questions, versus you answering theirs, or telling them what to do. What gets measured changes. Whatever the ratio, increase the percentage of "questions." Simple, all-purpose questions will do well: What do you think? How would you decide? What concerns would sway you one way versus the other?

3) Develop your social guidance system. In every interaction, practice all the nonverbal ways you can to match and mirror people, and lead toward a positive state: body posture, voice tone and tempo, energy level, facial expressions, breathing, criteria (clues they give in their language about what's important to them). These are all ways to align with others. Align before you lead. Observe what happens.

4) Add Personal Content. Start meetings with a "what's new in my world" round robin, just five minutes by the clock to give people a chance to report on something that's going on in their life. Make it upbeat, happy, fun – and anyone can skip if they want to. Find ways to bring laughter into meetings. Bring toys.

5) Under-commit. Use "I'll need to get back to you" more often – and then DO.

6) Listen. Allow people to feel heard without trying to solve their problems. It takes less time than you think. Stay quiet – it's a profound way to build trust.

– Section Two –
Grow through Cultivation
(Chapters 4-6)

The second truth we explore from nature is about cultivating conditions for strong growth. In a transparent Internet-driven global economy that has great variability, growth is fostered best by reducing control, increasing cooperation, and ensuring a LOT of effective communication between people.

Through stories of American soldiers effectively disarming a Muslim riot with nothing more than a smile, to a Navy pilot discussing communication in the cockpit during missions over Iraq, we see the power of communication and relationships in cultivating healthy growth and change.

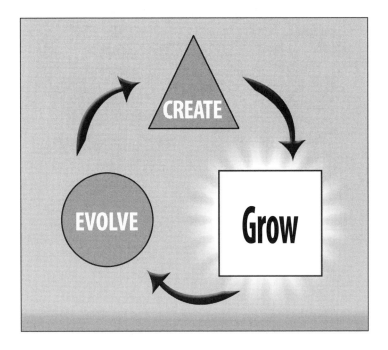

Chapter 4: GROWTH
The Structure of Growth Boundaries, Governance, and Guardrails

In Chapter 4, we explore how in nature, structure and governance interact with dynamic change, and explore how effective leaders set up good structures for planning, teamwork and decision making (guardrails and governance) as a framework that change can rest upon.

The Structure of Growth: Boundaries, Governance, and Guardrails

Nature's Truth #4:

In nature, structure and rules interact perfectly
with dynamic, constant change.

In business, structure and governance
need to create collaborative, empowered and
self-accountable workplaces.

*"The hardest thing in life is to know which bridge
to cross and which to burn."*

— David Russell

Some of the earth's oldest rock lies at the bottom of the Grand Canyon. Thousands of feet thick, monumental geologic forces lifted the rock up into a great range of mountains that were once thought to be equivalent to the height of the Himalayas (6 miles tall).

Over time, the mountains eroded into a plain. About one billion years ago, that plain was raised into a second mountain range. These mountains were then worn away by millions of years of rain, wind and frost.

During later ages, the entire region sank beneath an inland sea, with primitive shellfish fossilizing in sea bottoms that eventually hardened to shale. Eons later, the region rose again as a high plateau; the former sea bottom was now on top and the ancient rocks below.

The Colorado River went to work, first cutting into the upper layers about six million years ago. Carving inch by inch over the millennia, the river finally reached the oldest rocks nearly a mile below the surface.[16]

Sometimes called the "8th Wonder of the World," the Grand Canyon may be a surprising choice of metaphor in a book about fast-changing business environments. However, it provides a good perspective. In his book *How the Mighty Fall*, author and organizational change expert Jim Collins cites research showing that companies in the late stages of decline are characterized by panic, haste, radical change, hype and ever-narrowing options. The remedy? Calm, deliberate, disciplined practices that support steady change that can be digested and implemented effectively.

What can the steady regularity of the geologic process teach us about change? The uplift of the mountains (billions of years) followed by the erosion of the river (millions of years) created gigantic, awe inspiring results. If geologic forces had a coach, she would be saying: "Go slow (in the beginning) to go fast (later). The "Go Slow to Go Fast" principle is a central tenet of our work with change: When you create a structure up front to define a project or initiative clearly, it allows you to execute much faster.

A second lesson is the contrast of what changes and what does not. How water moves across a sloping surface does not change. It is driven by the laws of hydrology. The way the river cuts through the mesa is governed by the chemistry of water and mineral, and the mechanics of erosion. These laws of science are "guard rails" that define and determine the outcome of the process. They are a constant in the midst of much change.

In their haste to get moving, leaders often fail to spend adequate time up front preparing the system for change (go slow early to go fast later), and defining clear guardrails – boundary conditions. This chapter addresses both:

Nature's Guardrails: Clear goals and structure keep you focused and on track, but don't get caught in the goal trap!

The Nature of Governance: Ensure faster movement through the power of good decision making.

Nature's Guardrails

Six million years may seem a bit long compared to business timelines for getting a product to market or generating quarterly returns for Wall Street. But just pause for a moment and consider how this breathtaking example can show us the balance between what does and does *not* change.

Water's purpose is to flow. No matter what we try to do to stop it, water will seek its own level, cutting its path through the most unforgiving of resistance. This doesn't change. Its direction, destination and impact can change constantly. But water is *always* going to flow – that is its immutable law.

When we stop to realize that each part of nature has a set of fixed rules that guide its expression and evolution – even when we cannot always see those rules at work – this is a powerful and useful reminder for the process of leading change.

Birds migrate, yet there's no boss breathing down their neck to "get moving."

Trees drop their leaves in the Fall, yet there's no finger-pointing about whose fault it is that the tree won't produce profits for three months.

Tides roll in, tides roll out, yet nobody is pulling the strings on the moon.

Nature's boundary conditions are like guardrails — they make change easier. Remember, human beings didn't come with fixed guardrails. We got free will instead. This allows us greater choice than most of nature; it also carries a price of greater responsibility – and produces greater chaos. We can *choose* not to follow our encoded destiny, whatever it might be. We can (and do) consistently challenge, control and change the guardrails, or rules of engagement, of our natural world. We can literally move mountains – or just decide not to cooperate with the latest round of new initiatives and ideas.

When beginning a new venture in business (i.e., change) leaders rarely think to set up the guardrails for the team, or discuss the maintenance of the ones already in place. That's considered soft stuff that goes without saying. Once the plan is on paper and the announcement is made, "this is changing," it is assumed people will automatically create the proper guardrails to make it work.

At least that's the fantasy.

The reality is a bit different, for three specific reasons:

- Changes – even simple changes in routine – throw people off center, raising nuances and questions about how the new plan or initiative is different from the "old" vision, strategies and goals. People want to know: "What am I supposed to do differently, and why?" Rarely do leaders take time to link the change to a central, unchanging vision or purpose. Layers upon layers of small changes add up to a lot of confusion and burnout.

- Today's overly complex structures, systems and rules (designed based on a military environment, often assuming large size and scale) are filled with mixed messages about responsibility and roles: When am I empowered? How much am I empowered? Where does authority *really* reside? Who owns that decision? Each change adds another layer of confusion onto the onion.

- People are *maxed*. In an effort to "lean out" cost and compete on price, most businesses have fewer people to manage and do the work, with no meaningful reduction in workload and deliverables. Change is typically piled onto an already full plate but nothing is removed: What do I give up to make the time to do this new project? Projects are often assigned to the few "stars" whose existing workload is past capacity. Nothing is eliminated, and there is no budget to allocate new people to the project. Remember in our introduction, this is one of the top three reasons change efforts fail.

The Importance of Guardrails: Goals & Roles

We teach a team development course called *Collaborative Leadership Training (CLT)*. There is a moment near the beginning of this program when people in the class are often thinking "Why do I have to attend a class to learn how to run better meetings?" Good question. This is a thump in the head moment for most participants. Lack of clear goals plagues almost every change effort we've seen, small to huge. It seems so obvious, yet many leaders don't take enough time to make goals clear. As you read this section, you'll see us illustrate one of the most powerfully simple tools in the CLT program; GRPI. The letters stand for Goal, Role, Process and Interpersonal.

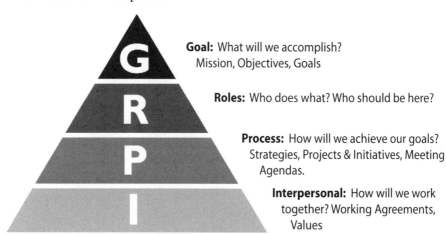

Goal: What will we accomplish?
Mission, Objectives, Goals

Roles: Who does what? Who should be here?

Process: How will we achieve our goals?
Strategies, Projects & Initiatives, Meeting Agendas.

Interpersonal: How will we work together? Working Agreements, Values

In this chapter, we speak in detail about Goals and Roles (P&I are very important, but not the topic of this chapter.)

How many meetings do you attend where the goal or purpose of the meeting is crystal clear? Most use an Agenda, but often do not define: "What is the objective or purpose of this meeting?" "What do we need to get done to finish this meeting?" Let's start at the top . . . .

Goals as Guardrails

Cathy was one of the few females who rose to the senior executive ranks at GE by the time she was 30. Since then, she has reinvented her career to help mid-sized companies plan their strategy. One day, we were discussing why leaders often resist setting and managing clear goals and other boundaries.

Her comment stayed with me: "Lack of a clear driving objective is the #1 missing link I see in businesses today. People working in an organization that lacks a clear definition of success don't have a beacon to draw them to the future, or to ensure they know whether they've succeeded or not. It's much easier to remain rooted in old ways of doing things when you are fuzzy about where you're headed."

In her view, there are three major weaknesses surrounding the lack of clear goals (a major guardrail) in teams and companies:

1. Lack of a clear target. Cathy described a small, privately held publishing company that had been losing money for seven years in one of their divisions. Cathy had been brought in to help them establish a plan for growth. In the past, they had no pressure to meet any of their numbers or specific revenue targets.

Early in the exploratory discussions, Cathy asked the senior team: "How do you define success?" Everyone was silent. Finally, the owner spoke up: "To be the leader." Cathy: "The leader of what?" Everyone again silent, looking at each other. Cathy said: "This is an 'aha moment' everyone! You are in a very competitive industry. You have to be able to distinguish yourselves. You have an educational program that is losing money, a publishing division that isn't growing, and an *idea* of sponsoring volun-tourism programs for existing customers. Defining success is important if you are going to change. Is "being the leader" #1 or #2 in market share? 20% annual revenue growth within each revenue stream? A specific revenue target – e.g., $10,000,000? The most common response (besides blank stares) was "We'll know success when we see it."

Finally, the CEO said: "It should be revenue."

Cathy: "OK, if it's $10,000,000 – where is it coming from?"

Response: "We just want to be #1 – our values and belief that we can is all we need."

The next day the CEO said to Cathy: "We don't want to waste any more of our time together talking about what success looks like. We will cover that in our managers' meeting."

It came as no surprise to Cathy that 18 months later, nothing had changed. The person running the business had not increased revenue, they hadn't made money, and they hadn't pursued any of the new opportunities they were aiming for. They were running on auto-pilot.

2. Getting the target to the people who will implement. Especially in mid-sized companies, it's very common for a leader to define: "these are our objectives" – but the news never gets communicated beyond the senior team.

For Cathy's clients, the strategic planning process begins with interviews — which include line employees. The conversation will often go something like this:

> C: Where do you stand on the company's strategic plan?
>
> Employee: What strategic plan?
>
> C: You have one, right?
>
> Employee: I've never seen it.

Then, the conversation with executives:

> C: Where do you stand on your strategic plan?
>
> Ex: We're on track to improve customer satisfaction. (No details about what it is today or what they want it to be.)
>
> C: Do employees in the call center know what that means?
>
> Ex: They don't really need to know. *We're* the ones working the plan.
>
> C: But the people who are responsible for executing your plan are in a different state. So how are they helping you improve customer satisfaction?
>
> Ex: Well, we're measuring how quickly they answer the call and how long they spend on the phone.

C: What are the plans to improve those behaviors?

Ex: We haven't worked out those details yet.

Senior managers often set goals and measurements, but the people implementing and being measured *have no idea* what the goals are, how success is defined, or that they are being measured on those behaviors.

Cathy advocates simplicity: "It's important to hone in on the metrics you need to help you make smart business decisions. In our call center example, if you measure, 'time to pick up the phone' and 'how much time on the phone with a client, the implied result is that the customer is being handled in an efficient manner. The reality is the employee is trying to get the customer off the phone. How many times does that customer have to call back? If they're calling in five times at 2-3 minutes per call, you haven't achieved any gain. You are far better off to measure problem resolution."

3. Setting up competing goals. Cathy says that far too often, the strategic planning process in companies is used to establish high-level aspirations for the business. When you drill deeper, you see that those plans have unwittingly set up internal competition. Sales says, "This is my target." Operations says "We can't execute on that." What next?

Executives rarely spend enough time discussing how their objectives can *support* each other and the whole business – which requires the team at the top to be collaborative and set clear priorities for the business: In today's complex environment this one task remains the most challenging (and usually least optimized) for any executive team.

This example points to a frequency in lack of clear direction, goals and objectives. Where are we going? How will we measure success? The GRPI model helps executives establish and cascade clear guardrails on projects and initiatives.

Too Much of a Good Thing? A Cautionary Note about Goals …

Goals are a good example of a "both-and" situation. In business, establishing them can become a rigid pastime that is more about checking the box than a dynamic planning process about what's really needed to move the business forward and remain competitive. Further, setting goals is de-motivating when you don't involve the people who will implement them in creating them, which is the secret to ownership and buy-in.

Visionary W. Edwards Deming pointed out that goals are great for organizing human attention but can easily become traps. He believed that highly specific, numerical and time-defined goals are the basis for performance reviews, employee rankings, short-term thinking, internal competition and office politics – all of which lead organizations to be more concerned with their survival than the quality of their products – i.e., these processes actually work *against* the systemic nature of a business, not in harmony with it. Goals create an artificial focus on quarterly reports, regional offices and organizational charts, and obscure the importance of treating a business as a complete and living human system.

On a more personal scale, when we set a goal and focus on it, we immediately limit ourselves in two ways: 1) We respond to all the opportunities of life and all the potentials within the limitation of that one single-pointed focus; and 2) As we move closer (or further away) from our consciously chosen goal(s) we measure our life by that goal instead of responding to the ever-changing world of possibilities around us.

In nature, goals "happen" naturally and shift constantly. In their book "Plans and the Structure of Behavior" even a single human nerve cell shows goal-oriented behavior.[17]

In the entire biological world, goals emerge, interact with one another, change, are satisfied (or not) and slip into the background as more urgent or current goals emerge. The point is to notice and become more conscious of the shifting and changing situation and respond to what's needed, versus what was happening last week or last year.[18]

So what's the final word on goals? Yes, as a business leader you need to clarify goals, define success, and be clear about the purpose behind what you are doing. We urge you to treat this concept more broadly than just making the most money possible. Remember, "the seed is the tree." The bigger your intention – and your desire to strike the right balance between profit, people, and purpose – the easier it is to create a workplace culture that is friendly to change and responsive to its environment.

Who's on First? The Importance of Defining Clear Roles

The second step in GRPI is to define roles. Sometimes we use this simple analogy in our Collaborative Leadership program:

Imagine you just adopted a new infant into your family. You already have three children, ages eight, six and four. Now you have a brand new member of the family. Will the change primarily be about buying a few new pieces of equipment and assigning new bedroom arrangements (the family version of technology systems and reorganizations)? Will telling your three children there's a new baby coming be enough to ensure that they know how to adjust their place in the family; be in relationship with the baby; and know what's expected of them now?

What would you do to effectively help make this adjustment in the family? Perhaps discuss new roles to help the baby's siblings who now have to compete for the diminished parental attention? Maybe the family needs to discuss new routines about who sleeps where (and when). The siblings will have a million questions, some of which parents won't know answers to. The change will require compromises on everyone's part about how the family spends time together. What else comes to mind?

This simple example is easy to translate into the business world: Whether or not you have children, you can imagine and appreciate unseen reactions and behaviors to a major change in the family system – and that will require considering the needs of the whole family, versus just attending to the infant's obvious demands.

In organizations, we often make changes that impact people's daily lives with callous disregard for the feelings and losses people experience, and provide very little time or attention to how to make it work. Where are the new guardrails? Leaders think because it's "just business" everyone will adapt and move on quickly.

The success of a business works best when it is managed as a *shared* responsibility. Leaders as authoritative parents and employees as children who feel entitled to get everything they wish for is no longer sufficient for today's complex, global workplaces. And it's not sustainable.

Whenever we facilitate our Role Alignment Process, groups want more time for the discussion. People are continuously confused about this territory in today's matrix structures, which slows (or in some cases paralyzes) decision making. The subject of role clarity and alignment deserves ongoing attention and the commitment to developing stronger connections and relationships across the boundaries and silos that exist.

If people are conflicted or confused, then it follows that one of the elements of G-R-P-I is not properly clarified. The GRPI model is a sound example of a guardrail that will keep organizations from slipping off the productivity track into the valley of irrelevant and inefficient process.

A small amount of experience using this tool shows big payoffs: Going slow at first definitely yields faster results later.

Almost every person spends too much time in meetings that waste time. A recent client implemented the GRPI tool in their meetings and found meetings became shorter and more focused – measurably. When you sit down for a few minutes to establish a GRPI for a meeting, you often find the meeting isn't needed and that there is a better way to accomplish the task. In any meeting that is spinning off track, or running long, a very effective move is to ask: "What is our goal right now?"

We encourage you to work with this one simple tool and watch what changes.

Roles of Leaders Sponsoring Change

There are different sponsoring roles during change, including executive sponsors and implementation sponsors. For executive sponsors, these are the most important responsibilities:

- **Set clear direction — work with your peers across the organization to achieve alignment.**

- Foster clarity and speed of decisions.

- Stay visible in sponsorship - attend regular team meetings.

- Meet regularly 1:1 with the team lead or champion and ask "What obstacles are you encountering and how can I help?" (And fix them.)

- Constantly ask three questions: What have you tried? What would you do differently? What have you learned?

Below is a complete version of the GRPI model with questions you can use to start aligning expectations and having shorter, more effective meetings – starting today.

Putting GRPI into Action

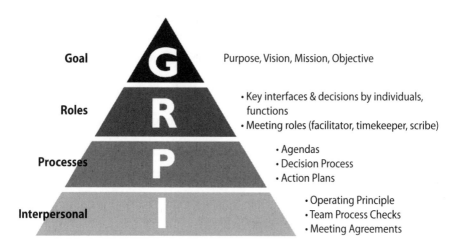

Goal	G	Purpose, Vision, Mission, Objective
Roles	R	• Key interfaces & decisions by individuals, functions • Meeting roles (facilitator, timekeeper, scribe)
Processes	P	• Agendas • Decision Process • Action Plans
Interpersonal	I	• Operating Principle • Team Process Checks • Meeting Agreements

Setting Structure: Powerful Questions

Below is a comprehensive menu of how to use GRPI to align expectations. Choose the ones that are most unclear for you today and start with aligning everyone toward a common understanding of those.

Goal – answers the questions:
   "WHY" are we doing this and "WHAT DOES SUCCESS LOOK LIKE?"

   • Why is this project important in the organization?

   • What are the expected outcomes and deliverables?

Roles – answers the questions:
   "WHO IS DOING WHAT" and "WHO SHOULD BE HERE?"

   • Who is the sponsor and what is the team's accountability to him or her?

   • What is each person's role and contribution to the team?

   • Why was each person selected?

Process – answers the question:
   "HOW WILL WE ACHIEVE OUR GOAL?"

   • How will we measure and track success? Report it? To whom?

   • What requirements or boundaries must the team work within?

   • How often will we meet . . . where . . . when?

   • What resources can we depend on? What will we need?

Interpersonal – answers the question:
   "HOW WILL WE WORK TOGETHER EFFECTIVELY?"

   • What will we do when we have disagreement/conflict?

   • What "working agreements" will support our relationships?

   • How will we discuss these when we forget or need to address exceptions?

The Nature of Governance: Decision Making & Decision Rights

During the early days of the second American invasion of Iraq, a group of soldiers set off for a local mosque to contact the town's chief cleric. Their goal was to ask his help in organizing the distribution of relief supplies. But a mob gathered, fearing the soldiers were coming to arrest their spiritual leader or destroy the mosque, a holy shrine.

Hundreds of devout Muslims surrounded the soldiers, waving their hands in the air and shouting, as they pressed in toward the heavily armed platoon. The Commanding Officer, Lieutenant Colonel Christopher Hughes, thought fast.

Picking up a loudspeaker he told his soldiers to "Take a knee," meaning to kneel on one knee.

Next he ordered them to point their rifles toward the ground.

Then his order was "Smile."

At that, the crowd's mood morphed. A few people were still yelling, but most were smiling in return. A few patted the soldiers on the back, as Hughes ordered them to walk slowly backward – away – still smiling.

That quick-witted move was the culmination of a dizzying array of split-second social calculations. Hughes had to read the level of hostility and assess what would calm them. He had to rely on the discipline of the men and their trust and obedience to his orders. And he had to gamble on hitting just the right gesture that would pierce the barriers of language and culture – all culminating in those split- second decisions.[19]

Your Brain on Decision Making

In nature, decisions are governed by a set of boundaries that are part of the system and a few simple criteria. Remember, water always flows – that's its nature. Whether it "decides" to curve left or right has to do with physics and gravity, not conscious choice. Although there are some examples of complex systems (such as ant and bee colonies), most of nature makes decisions based on a simple set of criteria:

1. Does it threaten or support my survival?

2. Does it provide a better opportunity for food or shelter?

3. **Does it give my offspring an advantage? (See #1)**

As we said before, human beings are unique from the rest of nature. We can make decisions to control our environment and destiny in ways other living parts of nature cannot (although most research will show our decisions come primarily from concerns about #1, 2 and 3, there is an additional element which we are wired to consider, which we call "service to others").

What carried Hughes through that tight spot with the Iraqis can be illustrated through the neural circuits inside the human brain – an interpersonal radar which has saved countless people in our human history and remains crucial to our survival even today.

How is this relevant to the everyday decisions we make about which employee to hire, whether to grow or expand, when to buy or sell?

Modern studies by neuroscientists provide increasingly relevant information about the way in which we *really* make decisions – the interplay between conscious, rational, analytical data and emotional, big- picture, systemic "gut feelings." You can now dissect the basis for the CEO's decision to *really* invest in a new opportunity or learn to predict whether you can trust a person to do the job you've hired them for.

The latest research shows us that over the past 100 years, with our growing dependency on technology and disconnection from the natural world (and the natural processes of survival), most of us are using a very limited capacity of what's possible to make decisions in our culture.

Speeding Up: When the River Narrows, the Water Moves Faster

In nature, when the banks of a river narrow, the water runs deeper and faster. This is a relevant parallel for organizations as well – if you want to move faster, narrow your focus on fewer priorities.

See if this scenario is familiar:

A meeting pops up on your Outlook calendar for this Thursday, a project review called by the top executive in the sales group. You hear through the grapevine that a key customer has expressed dissatisfaction about your team's work. There is no goal or agenda listed, just "project review." You show up early for the meeting, which begins 10 minutes past the appointed time (no way you'll make your next project session on time). The executive who called the meeting left town Wednesday morning for a last-minute fire drill. Instead of rescheduling, he sends his right hand (Joe) to conduct the session. After Joe conducts a rapid-fire Q&A in which most people provide vague answers and look down to avoid being called by name, the project team leader ends the pain by agreeing to "try" to bring the project in a full month earlier, as the customer has requested. You leave the meeting 10 minutes late, wondering: "Was there a decision made? What are we doing now? How are we going to actually meet that commitment and what other work will be set aside? What are the true priorities for my part of the business?"

And this is only one meeting of five you attend that day. The result is mind-numbing "do everything all-at-once" prioritization (or lack thereof). And the recent brain science research tells us that doesn't work very well.

In a fast-moving, customer-demand world of complexity, organizations are struggling under pressures like this every day. It's imperative for managers and employees to stop believing that being the "boss" means you have the answer – and start getting clear and focused about what's most important and who should decide. Bosses increasingly should NOT believe they have the answer, but need to see their role as effectively, and rapidly, *facilitating* solutions to the problems that arise based on two central outcomes: (1) reducing and narrowing the pathway to achieving clear objectives; and (2) using customers' feedback about how you can be more valuable to them.

A cardinal rule in software development is to manage the backlog of work and relentlessly control to a small list of tasks that are active – to minimize "context-switching." There are measures that show that as soon as you have more than two tasks, your effectiveness is dramatically reduced. In his book "*Your Brain at Work*" David Rock[20] refers to this as "dual-task interference." In a famous experiment in the 1980's, Harold Pashler showed when people do two cognitive tasks at once, their cognitive capacity can drop from that of a Harvard MBA to that of an eight-year-old.

Due to stress, time constraints and deeply held mindsets about authority, appropriate decisions about prioritization rarely happen. This is one important cause of why change efforts gain so little traction and buy-in. Solutions do not make sense to people because their fingerprints are literally not on the work, but also because the version of the plan that looks so logical on paper, rarely considers how to effectively change the existing workload, challenges and constraints of the people who will implement it.

Better Decisions: What You Don't Think About

Another element of making better decisions faster is to stop relying on a ½-brained decision process. Literally. Effective, fast decision making involves the entire capacity of the human brain:

Left Hemisphere	Right Hemisphere
Logic	Intuition
Facts, #'s	Meaning
Function	Aesthetic
Sequential	Simultaneous
Text (language)	Context (pictures, video)
Analysis	Synthesis
Aware – known and certain	Unaware – unknown, uncertain, not thought about
Limited point of view, self, my department	Empathy, broad points of view

According to the neurologist Antonio Damasio,[21] the seat of our conscious thought (the prefrontal cortex) has a reciprocal connection with the emotion-gathering amygdala, ensuring that we don't make decisions with objective logic (despite our belief that we do). In fact, he conducted an ingenious experiment proving that if we did rely on our conscious thought process, we'd make bad decisions.

In his experiment, a subject is given $2,000 of play money to make wagers on the results of turning over a card from one of four decks labeled A, B, C, and D. The subject is not told how long the game will last, but each card will either result in earning or losing money. The given payoffs or costs are disclosed only after the turn of the card. The cards in decks A and B either win $100 or lose as much as $1,250. Those in decks B and C pay $50, but lose only up to $100.

Normal players sample all four decks and early-on show an initial preference for A and B and their larger payoffs. After a while, however, they shift to C and D, apparently recognizing the high risk of the A and B decks. However, patients with lesions in the ventromedial area of the prefrontal cortex showed a sustained preference for the high risk A and B decks, even as their losses bankrupted them.

Damasio hypothesizes that the patients with the lesions had lost the ability to anticipate and plan for the future. Instead, they were ruled by the now. This ability to plan for the future has to do with what Damasio calls somatic markers. After trial and error, normal patients learned to associate a selection from decks A and B with a feeling of "badness." This feeling biased them away from choosing those two decks. The ventromedial area is, as you might expect, connected to the amygdale.

In a follow-up experiment, the game was played with subjects who had their skin conductive response measured, as in a lie detector test. Prior to the selection of the deck, normal patients experienced an increase in the magnitude of the response, and the magnitude continued to grow as the game continued. In other words, the prediction of "badness" from decks A and B was made unconsciously before the conscious decision of which deck to select was made. Emotions drove the prediction.

These findings explain how we actually make decisions. Our past experiences carry an emotional charge that is encoded in memories. When we encounter a situation similar enough to summon up those past experiences, along with their associated emotions, our prospective choices are marked by those emotions. We, then, are motivated to choose the ones that are "good" versus the ones that are "bad." This means that the more we attempt to strip out feelings and create an objective decision-making process, the more we lose access to what we have learned from past experiences.

While conventional wisdom holds that "I" consciously solve problems and make decisions, the results of this experiment suggest otherwise. I become aware of the solution or the decision when it has already been arrived at through processes that are not conscious. Perhaps even more counterintuitive is that emotions, not logic, drive the decision-making process. The ideal of decision making in the corporate world – rigorous objectivity – virtually ensures the loss of what's been learned through experience It appears that it isn't the pressure from Wall Street for quarterly results that prevents an adequate long-term perspective, but our preference for supposedly objective thinking.

The results of Damasio's experiment make it clear that we're not reasoning the way we think we are. Mental processes we're not conscious of drive our decision making, while the kind of logical reasoning we believe our thinking should aspire to is really no more than a way to justify the decisions we have already made. But it's not just our own thinking that is at issue. If we use logic to influence people unconsciously driven by emotion, we probably aren't going to be very successful in getting them to embrace our point of view.[22]

This research supports the process outlined in Chapter 2, about the use of leadership "storytelling" to elicit emotion, create meaning, paint a picture and demonstrate empathy (all right brain activities). This is *in addition to* (not instead of) the use of PowerPoint to share facts, educate about numbers, and provide analysis (feeding the left brain). This is another example of the need for *both-and* leadership.

Decision Rights Versus Nagging Rights

One of the central trademarks of our work with executives and their teams is a process to clarify what decision rights they should own (see Chapter 5 for a detailed description). This is "my place in the sandbox" territory. The evidence of poor decision making usually can be found by talking to the shared service groups in any business who are inundated with requests from the business lines (IT, HR, Product Development, Project Management).When no coordination has happened at the top, the trickle-down situation becomes a living nightmare for mid-level executives who are constantly being asked to perform miracles by delivering better results and finish more projects for less money.

The CEO of a legacy company in the publishing industry was undergoing a painful and critical strategic shift in their business model. As an organization that held 70% market share, operating with unclear and luxurious decision cycles didn't impact the business much. In our work with him and his team, it became clear that decision rights was the central issue that was keeping his team from being able to speed up their business. As a self-described "bungee jumper" he often meddled in the decisions that should have been owned by his team.

Eventually, the CEO undertook a disciplined process of defining what decisions he held for the business:

- **The vision and values of our business**

- **What businesses we are in, and what to invest in**

- **The organizational structure**

- **Fostering a competitive organizational culture**

Everything else he claimed as "nagging rights." While this may seem simplistic, it took him four years to come to this level of clarity! By his being explicit, it created a very powerful discussion among his team, and eventually cascaded to the next two levels of managers – all of whom needed to think through the same topics.

For Dan, Bill and Charles in our technology company, decision rights was a central problem because the organization's structure was very specialized and silo-d. The sales organization was allowed to regularly insert their opinions and requests into the engineering process very late. The term "infinite appeal" was used to describe the phenomenon that any decision could be revisited and reversed, at any time. This was a primary cause of software release delays. In addition to facilitating a version of our decision process, we provided a common language for the roles necessary to continuously establish clear decision rights:

Bungee-Jumping, *defined:*

- o Retracting or reversing decisions made by your direct report regarding a customer or team, without coaching or explanation;

- o Making agreements or promises directly to or through someone below your direct report;

- o Making decisions outside your boundaries.

Bungee jumping creates co-dependency, dis-empowers people, and erodes trust by hijacking decisions.

Nagging rights, *defined:*

Senior execs typically get to their level by being the best critical thinkers, i.e., by thinking more sharply and clearly than others. They need to develop others to do the same by:

- o Coaching and facilitating better decisions;

- o Helping others think more clearly and sharply by asking hard questions and making decision criteria explicit;

- o Pushing decisions closer to the customer or action;

- o Engaging in a feedback process requiring dialogue to improve the speed and quality of decisions.

Masterful nagging (influencing or coaching) is the antidote to bungee-jumping.

Blocking, *defined:*

Slowing progress on another team by escalating, aka Reverse Bungee-Jumping. It is caused by someone disagreeing with a decision and escalating to a more senior person to try to get his or her way. The antidote is collaboration: have a direct, honest conversation with the person who represents the point of view in question. When that doesn't work, the best strategy is to set a short meeting and discuss it together in real-time, versus allowing email disintegration to suck hours of time and escalate misunderstanding. This strategy also avoids the need for 100% consensus, explicitly agreeing there is ONE agreed-upon decision maker; that important people have weighed in to support that ONE person's decision; and those people will not appeal it.

To speed up decision making, you must address the territory of WHO decides what, and create a sound decision process. This will help to overcome the confusion that plagues teams, projects and goals, which shows up in questions like: "Was there a decision?" "Who makes the decision?" "Do we *really* need consensus?"

In most organizations, the pendulum has swung from "total control" to "too much consensus." When it comes to change, there is an art form to finding the balance between structure (control) and freedom (everyone has a say). In our work, we are typically advising executives support fewer opinions and provide more clarity of structure. This helps people find focus and execute better. If you remember the Go Slow to Go Fast principle and apply good decision making structure, you will find the pendulum can rest in its proper state of balance.

SUMMARY
Nature's Truth #4

In business, structure and governance need to create collaborative, empowered and self-accountable workplaces. That leads to better results: Fruit!

Placing your attention on a few key guard rails in the beginning may seem to slow you down, however getting everyone aligned about the critical boundaries will speed you up for the long haul. "Go slow to go fast."

- Setting clear goals and creating commitment to them rarely involves the right people. Although the final authority should reside with one person, it's too often a one-way conversation in business.

- A leader's role is to relentlessly narrow and help prioritize during change – "Where the river narrows, the water moves faster."

- Use GRPI – or your preferred model – to establish clear guardrails during change.

- Remember emotion is at least as important as logic in deciding.

- Clarify Decision Rights in contrast to Nagging Rights.

- Implement a good decision making process (see "Making it Work").

Making It Work! Small Changes for Improving Decision Making

In addition to using GRPI as a planning model for building a solid framework to support your seeds of growth (meetings, initiatives, project planning), following are excerpts from our decision practices model to address the most common decision derailers in projects:

1) **What's the goal of the decision?** A clear definition of success is crucial. Often it's fuzzy, not stated, or not visible. If the decision maker can't decide, the first place to look for clarity is: "What's the goal?"

2) **Who is the decision maker?** There is only ONE. That's the first rule. Often that person is not defined, or it's defined but not known. Often the decision is being made 1-2 levels higher than it should. And, often, the person making the decision is absent from the meeting where the group is trying to decide or has sent a scout ("I'm too busy"). Reschedule the meeting if that person is missing, and the goal of the meeting is to make the decision. It's just a waste of everyone's time.

3) **How will we decide?** Prioritize the decision criteria:
Will this advance us toward our objective or be a distraction? Who else is this going to impact? And how?
What could be the most likely misinterpretation; how do we avoid that. Will it seem fair?
Does this decision build and support trust or erode it? Can we trust the implementation team?
Does this help our business grow and learn?
You will make better decisions by choosing your top two criteria and prioritizing the others behind those. It's impossible for the brain to track three courses of action (or priorities). For example, if you are

going to make a trade-off on requirements for a new software platform, you have to meet quality, cost and development timelines. If you have absolute criteria on time, then choose between quality or cost and assume the 3rd is your lowest priority for NOW—and bring it into line later.

4) **Allow soak time – but not too much!** You need to let important decisions marinate – remember the power of your unconscious process. "Let me sleep on it, I'll come back to you tomorrow... or by the end of the week" is a good answer, more of the time. Then DECIDE and stop second-guessing.

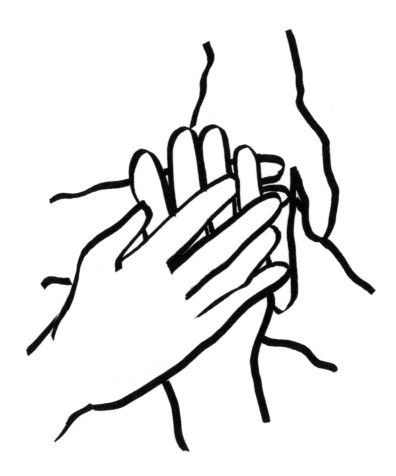

Chapter 5: COLLABORATE
Power-Up the Tribe!

Chapter 5 explores the tribal model of collaboration, and how to apply this to business. Leaders who do so are masterful at engaging and involving more people sooner – employees, key influencers, suppliers, competitors. This provides a contrast to the outdated "Industrial Age" management paradigm, to restore the natural balance of personal accountability and create better methods for understanding and handling conflict.

Power-Up the Tribe!

Nature's Truth #5:

In nature, everything is part of an interactive system.

In business, artificial boundaries must be
dissolved to foster interaction and cooperation,
which produces more rapid adaptation

*"Human beings can't help it: We need to belong. One
of the most powerful of our survival mechanisms is
to be part of a tribe, to contribute (and take from)
a group of like-minded people. We are drawn to
leaders and to their ideas, and we can't resist the
rush of belonging and the thrill of the new."*

— Seth Godin, Tribes

Imagine: Africa about the year 50,000 B.C.

We were living in the savannahs, hunting for meat, gathering berries, and otherwise looking like any other group of two-legged apes once common in Africa.
But something was different about us: We decorated and adorned our bodies like
humans do; we created art like humans do; we planned our hunting and gathering
like humans do; and, most importantly, we improved on everything we did and

taught our children everything we knew in the hopes that their lives would be better. Nobody yet knows what made us different from the other apes—perhaps it was a combination of seeking new ideas and having the language to communicate those ideas to others—but whatever happened so many years ago in Africa made us human. And that's when our story starts.

There were only a few thousand of us back then. All of humanity could have fit into a ballpark. Every day under the burning sun the men hunted while the women collected berries and nuts. Every night under the brilliant stars we huddled together and told ourselves stories. Sometimes we were afraid, when the storms washed the land, or when a lion came to hunt, but we knew where to hide and we knew how to fight and every day we learned new things.

There were only a few thousand of us back then, but every century there were more of us.[23]

Human Population Growth Since 1 A.D.

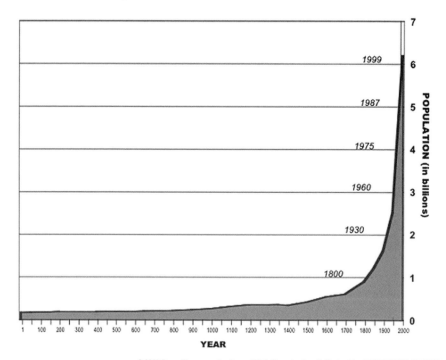

© 2000 Bruce Thompson, EcoTracs, 937 E. Browning Ave. Salt Lake City, UT 84105 (801) 467-3240

9 billion people on the planet in 2050?!
The question we are wondering is: How will we all get along?

The human tribe. Our source of kinship, survival, emotional happiness, and comfort.

As cultures and sub-cultures collide in a global melting pot of ancestry, history, and customs, our DNA is still tied to the power of the tribe. Our workplaces are filled with modern versions of basic tribal rituals: Hunting. Gathering. Storytelling. Loyalty. Cooperation. Conflict.

The innovations of a post-modern society – agriculture, science, technology, and global interactivity – have not fundamentally changed the fact that we are at our best when organized in a small band of 20-40 people who are collectively responsible for their survival and well-being.

We can take a lesson from this in our modern workplaces. Whether you are leading in an entrepreneurial company, a large corporation, a community non-profit or a church there is a clear structure to how you build self-responsible effective groups to accomplish something great. We call that structure collaborative leadership, and it is the central element of our work for creating more adaptive, fast moving teams and organizations.

It is grounded in a simple principle.

The Fingerprint Test

If you want people to OWN the work,
You must create a process for them to DO the work.
Whose fingerprints are on the work?
If it's not the people who will implement, you won't
have commitment or ownership.

As we learn skills to make adapting to change easier and more effective, we can draw lessons that guided thousands of years of human history within the tribal system.

But first, let's look at how we took a different path, and got ourselves a bit off-track.

Fast forward about 51,898 years.

It's 1898 – the year Frederick Winslow Taylor joined Bethlehem Steel.

Taylor is the man responsible for how we manage in our modern world – largely due to the common shovel.

Peter Drucker ranked Taylor's effect on our modern world with that of Sigmund Freud and Charles Darwin.

During his time at Bethlehem Steel, Taylor was given the task of designing a more efficient shovel for men to load coal into blast furnaces. He approached this job like any good scientist of the Industrial Age: measuring, observing, and calculating the minute actions and results of the men as they worked throughout the day. He experimented with differing amounts of coal per shovelful, and found that twenty-one and a half pounds was the exact amount to ensure the men worked efficiently all day and moved the most coal. When he redesigned the shovel to hold that amount, the company was able to reduce the number of men shoveling coal from 500 to 140.

But he didn't stop there. Taylor realized the design of the shovel was only a part of the productivity equation. The other part was how the men *used* the shovel. Applying the same approach he used to improve the efficiency of machines to the people working *on* the machines, Taylor broke the task down into its component parts, made careful measurements, and concluded there was "one right way" to shovel the coal. He taught all of the men to shovel that way, and there was another significant increase in productivity.

Thus marked the dawn of the "efficiency and productivity" movement that would become known as Scientific Management. And, this also marked the demise of the "freedom and responsibility" of workers.

Prior to the Industrial Age, men in factories came from a lineage of craftsmen who took pride in their skill and independence. Suddenly, they were stripped of the responsibility to think. With Frederick Taylor and Scientific Management as the paradigm, young men with college educations and stopwatches determined how work was to be done – not the people who actually had the experience doing the work.

Relationships, creativity, or thinking were of no importance. What mattered was following the process laid out, exactly as prescribed. By reducing men to a "cog in a machine," in the words of Samuel Gompers of the AFL, business got what it asked for: a relentless drive toward efficiency. The consequence? An about-face of personal responsibility and the creation of adversarial relationships between managers and employees.

It was the precursor to a specialist business model that has "divided the worm into several pieces, expecting that each will separately find its way to the food source." [24]

Fast Forward 112 (Or So) Years.

It's 2010. The world is flatter, faster, and more complex.

Scientists for the Industrial Age saw the universe operating according to linear rules of cause and effect. If you hit a billiard ball, you could measure its speed and trajectory and predict where it will stop with a high degree of accuracy. If you made a person's pay dependent on their rate of production, they could be expected to work harder (although they actually didn't). The universe was one big machine – if you disassembled the machine, you would understand the whole. If the universe's components were just part of a machine, by working to make each part better, the *whole* would work better. By this logic, the universe and everything in it could be predicted and controlled.

Anyone who has raised children, worked on a farm, or managed the Millennial generation in the workforce can see this belief is limited. Cause-effect in nature is a complex interaction of many variables, seen and unseen. It can be illustrated better as a spider web in which many parts of the whole are interconnected, versus a linear model.

Companies trapped in a simplistic mindset of "managers have answers; workers are here to comply" are seeing their efforts to adapt and change hitting a brick wall.

Need evidence? Companies spend billions of dollars on Lean, Business Process Simplification, and Six Sigma – evidence that Peter Drucker didn't exaggerate Taylor's impact. One software development manager states it perfectly: "We have too many of these kinds of programs that are good in their conception, but don't stick because people don't see the reason to make the changes in their daily habits." After decades of attempts to restore greater responsibility and empowerment to non-management ranks, 2 out of 3 people inside organizations today do not *naturally* come to work feeling empowered, free to make decisions, engaged fully with their head *and* heart, with the permission to raise questions or concerns. [reference Gallup, get from Intro]

Recently, Lisa was traveling from Denver to the East Coast when a blizzard shut down the Denver airport. The next day she was due to speak to a group in South Carolina. Needless to say, this created some stress. She managed to rebook on a red-eye flight which departed Denver at 1:00 AM with a small window to catch a connecting flight from Atlanta at 7:30 a.m., which meant she could still arrive at her engagement on time. But the plane was held in Denver to allow some passengers from another cancelled flight to come on-board. By the time it arrived in Atlanta, she had 18 minutes to make the connecting flight on a different concourse. The minutes ticked by in agony as she watched the flight attendant usher the entire first class cabin off the plane first (after an announcement requesting people wait for passengers trying to make connections). Once off the plane, she asked the gate attendant: "Would you please call the gate agent for my flight and ask them to hold the flight a few minutes?" (Given the flight she had just taken was held for others and her connection was a commuter flight, this seemed reasonable.) The gate agent's response? "I can't do that." (To which Lisa replied, "Of course you *can*.

You *won't*.") After a high-speed airport sprint, Lisa arrived at the departing gate 1 minute after they had closed the doors. She ended up on a flight 2.5 hours later, missing her speaking engagement in Charleston.

Everyone has a story of service professionals who are blind and apathetic to the very reason they exist: to help solve people's problems.

This simple analogy illustrates the problem of using Taylor-era management to navigate a complex, transformational world. The separation of the "brain" from the "body" means that leaders, customers, and employees no longer see themselves in pursuit of a common purpose. With some exceptions, organizational change efforts do not fail from lack of tools to manage process, spreadsheets, or projects. They fail because leaders do not effectively tap into the innate desire to work together, to get things done *and* to serve one another's best interests. On top of that, we have so many tribes with so many different customs (four generations, ten countries, six functional disciplines) trying to work in harmony – with an uninspired goal of making more money for a separate entity most of us have never met.

Building relationship is the container in which every change effort succeeds or fails. *No exceptions*. We do not exist unto ourselves. With rare exceptions, we cannot even stay *alive* in our modern society without help from others. (Where does your food and water come from?) The structures that evolved from the paradigm of boss over employee are unnatural – and completely override human tribal wisdom that fosters responsibility, the desire to "learn something new every day" and the drive to "become the best we can be." This is the model that reminds us that we are in relationship with each other and the natural world, and creates a sense of harmony with that system.

We must actively work to recast deeply entrenched mindsets from the Industrial Age into management practices and systems that ignite shared responsibility and connection.

Collaboration is the business mechanism for doing this. It is a framework and a justification for leaders to connect people more consciously to one another and to a bigger picture. Collaborative leadership ensures that during change initiatives, proper attention is paid to people and relationships. This is not easy for today's leaders because it goes directly against the grain of everything we have learned and known as long as any of us have been alive (thanks in part to Frederick Taylor). But we can already see examples of conscious, courageous, and patient leaders paving the way.

In his book *"The Whole New Mind,"* Daniel Pink calls our current era "The Conceptual Age," marked by affluence, automation, and powerful technological progress. He poses three chilling questions that every American leader would be well-advised to consider:

1) Can someone overseas do it cheaper?

2) Can a computer do it faster?

3) Is what I'm offering in demand in an age of abundance?

Every organization today – whether you are a non-profit, government, entrepreneurial or corporate entity, faces the reality of a global, competitive world in which knowledge work is king and can be done in China for a fraction of the cost in the U.S. The core competency of learning how to change and adapt rapidly and gracefully *will* become the litmus test of who survives and who goes extinct in the coming decades. It requires collaboration, because in a complex world, no one person *has* the best answers. This is not about returning to the primitive nature of tribes or the controlling nature of industrial management, but drawing from the best of both worlds: the primitive wisdom of the learning to work in small tribes that self-organize, share accountability, and cooperate AND the industrial management model of the ability to be efficient and effective PLUS the modern importance of purpose, meaning, and connection.

The question is how.

Building More Collaboration

Remember the fingerprint test: "If you want people to own the work, create a process for them to do the work" – to get their fingerprints on important decisions about the work. One of the key collaborative leadership principles sets the stage to create more fingerprints on the work, a continuum between content expert and process facilitator:

Content Expert
Tell, Teach, Advocate

Process Facilitator
Ask, Explore, Inquire

Let's illustrate where you fall on this continuum with a simple example. When you consider the range of meetings you've attended over the years, the type of behavior of the person leading the meeting falls into two distinct categories:

- Content expert

- Process facilitator

When the Content Expert is running the meeting, what do you notice? Typically he is talking, providing information, there is little interaction, and the conversation is "one way" – them to the audience. This is useful for transferring lots of information quickly; however there is not much buy-in or commitment. You can summarize this end of the continuum as TELL.

When a pure Facilitator is running the meeting, there is more interaction, she is eliciting information, and there is lots of dialogue. This usually results in more ownership, more points of view; however it initially takes longer (although can be faster long term). You can summarize this end of the continuum as ASK.

In our collaborative leadership training, we ask managers to rate themselves on the continuum: Where are you most comfortable? Usually it is close to the TELL side.

Most leaders understand that more engagement, ownership and better results happen by engaging in a dialogue versus a monologue. In the training, leaders are given a task to facilitate a meeting in which they must consciously spend most of their time asking questions of the group, and "tell" less. Their segment of the meeting is captured on video. Most are surprised after watching their video clip, that the majority of their time was spent TELLING, not ASKING. Most leaders *think* they engage and facilitate dialogue more than they do – and when challenged, say "I don't have time." When you literally record the time difference, you find it's often a matter of investing a few minutes to engage in a brief dialogue – which saves huge amounts of time trying to back-pedal to overcome resistance to change. This point is NOT to be confused as "consensus" or group decision making: As a leader you can and should) retain decision rights, at the same time that you create more buy-in by facilitating a dialogue and process by which people feel heard and understood.

How can we bring tribal wisdom into the modern age? Tribes had clear structures for accountability, decision making, and order. The survival of the clan depended on it. We draw two central concepts from the tribal model as lessons for modern organizations:

Cooperation v. Competition – The ability to know and face your real competition, and cooperate where it's most needed: inside your own company.

Accountability and Conflict – Helping people remember their natural state of self-responsibility and clarity of individual purpose, which have been obscured by Industrial Age management practices.

Cooperation v. Competition

"We have met the enemy and he is us."

— **Walt Kelly.**

"Us" versus "them" is as old as the Stone Age. People have engaged in conflict as long as we have been on the planet.

In most cases, conflict among people was an external threat – a predator whom the tribe competed with for resources. The tribe itself was usually a sanctuary of shared purpose and cooperation. Everyone understood their roles and was accountable to the tribe. Many tribes were truly egalitarian in nature, which meant everyone belonged and was accepted, and nobody had to endure loneliness or isolation unless they violated the norms of the tribe and were outcast. (Our Constitution says we believe it, but if we're really honest, we have a ways to go).

Today – especially in our American society – "us" is really "me." The rugged individualistic culture usurps true cooperation. For example, reward and incentive systems that favor the individual over the team are a deeply ingrained mindset in many organizational cultures. We can even see this within our own family systems, with siblings competing for attention. Often, within teams you will see leaders unwittingly pit people against one another even when they share common interests and it is in their best interests to cooperate.

Gerry lives in a beach town where the unchecked development of beachfront property is rampant. There are people building houses directly on top of the fragile dune ecosystem – the very structure nature uses to protect the land. Without the dunes, the island will eventually erode and the homes will literally float to sea. The town government finally put a moratorium on the building - *after* several homes were erected right on top of the dunes. Yet, the developers and owners are fighting back: As owner of their little piece of land, they believe they have the "right" to build wherever they want — at the expense of their neighbors and the ecosystem that makes the place enjoyable; and, ironically, endangering their own house. (God help them when the first hurricane blows through.)

Land developers are seen as the enemy of natural resources and the people who are already living on the land. And yet, these three "systems" – the builders, the animals/plants, and the current residents – do not really need to *compete* for resources. This false competition has been set up because people have decided cooperation means "selling out." The root cause? An unwillingness on the part of these "special interest groups" to give up their individual needs, desires, or mindsets and find a way that everyone can benefit from and protect this fragile natural ecosystem.

An example closer to your home: In the Industrial Age, organizations created specialization. The result was what are commonly known as "silos" – bands of mini-tribes organized as a business unit (delivering a type of product or service) or a functional area (performing a specific service to support the products and services). In an effort to coordinate these specialized functions, we have attempted to connect people across the silos by creating "the matrix." But anyone who has tried to work in one knows they aren't as effective as everyone hoped. One reason is because the structure *assumes* a level of cooperation and relationship which doesn't exist. Modern organizations are plagued by internal "fiefdoms" and territory wars that over-emphasize individual rights. People in most modern organizations act as though there is a finite amount of organizational resources (people, money, promotions, glory, attention) and each leader of the "business unit tribe" or the "functional tribe" or the "department tribe" must fight for their share. Leaders rarely work together to create "shared goals" that ensure the people below them can implement without competing for resources or priorities. This mindset results in cannibalizing the organization's true common interests.

While everyone is busy fighting one another, the *real* threat – the predators called your competition – are given more peripheral attention. (Case in point: How many employees in your company can name the top three direct competitors to your organization?) Because people are competing with each other for attention inside their tribe, they don't see the lion in the bushes waiting to pounce.

Internal competition for resources, attention, power, and glory is like driving with one foot on the gas pedal and one on the brakes – hindering innovation (top line growth) and efficiency (profitability).

Leaders who want to create more adaptable organizations must focus on cultivating their tribe's cooperation in its best expression by building a sense of shared "common purpose" and responsibility to one another; and connecting people across functional and geographical boundaries.

That's how you survive and ensure your tribe grows.

Modern Tribes: The Aboriginal World View

- Hunter-gatherers work 12-20 hours a week. For part of the year they do not have to work at all. They have much free time for creating art, oral literature, music, and dance.

- Most are peaceful people – often they do not even have a word for war.

- Hunter-gatherer society's demand every hunter share his kill. Sharing is a food storage system because sharing with others earns the right to be repaid at some future time.

- Bushmen spend much of their free time visiting to keep up friendships. They talk about hunting, the weather, distributing food, gift-giving, and scandal.

- Arguments are interesting. Bushmen argue about unfair sharing, selfishness in gift-giving, and the failure to offer good hospitality. They get angry and then, suddenly, without either person seeming to give in, the fight is over. A few minutes later, the participants are chatting and laughing together.

- Bushmen would rather leave than risk a physical confrontation. Hunter-gatherers are afraid of violence because they know it can destroy a small group.

- Bushmen do not honor fighting and aggression. They have no stories of bravery, praise for aggressive manhood, ordeals of strengths, or competitive sports.[25]

How does this world view compare to your organization?

Accountability and Conflict

It would be incomplete to discuss the power of tribes without discussing the importance of accountability and conflict management.

Accountability in a tribal system is based on adherence to customs and oral teachings of tribal elders that support the whole of the community – versus compliance to a powerful boss. While governance is important to keep order within a group, focusing on individual wholeness and fostering a state in which each person can remember and act from their natural state of personal accountability is a very compelling proposition for leaders who are struggling with this issue in their companies. Examples abound of young employees who may never have had a job and don't even know to show up on time to meetings (we heard one example of an employee who waited for her boss to come get her as a reason she hadn't attended the regular staff meeting), to the entitled executive who rests on past wins and leaves a train wreck of relationships … and the company keeps passing him around even though he doesn't get results.

Why do organizations tolerate this lack of personal accountability?

What's your theory about the answer? Think about it.

Our theory is simple: It is uncomfortable and unfamiliar territory to hold people accountable, because it also requires you to *be* accountable. You can't walk the talk if you're not willing to demonstrate it yourself. This situation is compounded by Peter Drucker's observation that Scientific Management permeates every aspect of our culture: personal accountability is not popular because that's the responsibility of the guys who held the clipboards. "You want me to be proactive and think? You aren't paying me enough and you didn't give me the title." Not all employees think this way, but too many who have tried, have been shut down with the inference "That's not your job." Remember in Chapter 3 when we spoke about the source of mistrust is often leaders who shut down people who stick their necks out and make suggestions? We've created brick walls of misunderstanding in our workplaces – and these need to be broken down with thought and care.

Rather than resolving conflict and producing accountability, an over-dependence on managers as the keeper of decisions and finder of fault has actually *escalated* conflict and *reduced* accountability. What was intended to simplify governance and create compliance and order has created rampant mistrust, non-thinkers, and non-responsibility. A true remedy to this feels far too difficult for organizations to tackle – like building a high-rise when you have never lifted a hammer.

But the reality is good news: awakening people to their natural state - in which they want to be self-directed and do well - is *not* that difficult. It takes a few small changes in how you communicate and manage people – and some patience and persistence. Not *everyone* will respond, but enough do to make the practice worthwhile.

Consider this tribal example of how you might re-think conflict and mistakes in your organization as one step toward improving individual accountability:

How We Used to Handle Conflict

The indigenous justice paradigm is based on the world view of the aboriginal inhabitants of North America. They view crime as a natural human error that requires corrective intervention by families and elders or tribal leaders. Offenders remain an integral part of the community because of their important role in defining the boundaries of appropriate and inappropriate behavior, and the consequences associated with misconduct.

The victim is the focal point, and the goal is to heal and renew the victim's physical, emotional, mental, and spiritual well-being. It also involves deliberate acts by the offender to regain dignity and trust, and to return to a healthy physical, emotional, mental, and spiritual state. To repair relationships, it is essential for the offender to make amends through apology, asking forgiveness, making restitution, and engaging in acts that demonstrate a sincerity to make things right. These are necessary for the offender and victim to save face and to restore personal and communal harmony.[26]

It's powerful to consider what would happen in our American business if we restored a tribal definition and process to encourage accountability. While it takes a mature viewpoint, we have no doubt that millions of dollars could be saved on conflict resolution, accountability programs, and mediation if the story below became the dominant spirit for how people thought about their responsibility and role, and handled disagreements.

The Plywood Artwork

In the summer of 1992, Gerry was teaching a 20-day residential training program for change agents in the Rocky Mountains in Winter Park, Colorado. A group of 75 people had bonded strongly during the three-week program. And as part of their experience, they had created a large piece of visual artwork which became a symbol of their community. The finished product was a collaborative painting representing their experiences together. It was painted with red, white, black, and yellow to symbolize all the people of the earth, and it was filled with a collage of handprints and spirals, yin-yang. It included individual contributions from every participant. It was very meaningful to everyone.

It was the closing hour of the program and one task remained: "What are we going to do with this piece of art?" The majority of the participants felt it should be kept safe and given to somebody who would be the custodian. But still unanswered was: "How are we going to facilitate the who, the how and the where?" The community included people from all over the world and it was a VERY large piece of plywood.

Then one man spoke up.

"Well," he said, "because this is so challenging, and because we're spread out all over the planet—with people from Europe and Asia—my proposal is that we destroy it. If we burn it, it will be like *everybody* has it."

The tension in the room mounted instantly. It was clear the group was generally quite opposed to the idea of destroying it. To most of them, burning the artwork would seem like a great offense to what it represented. The man who had offered the suggestion was thinking on a more abstract level, but most people wanted to keep this piece of art that represented the close-knit community they had formed over the past weeks. They did not want it destroyed.

It was the end of 20 days, and everyone was tired and ready to leave. I was trying to facilitate the conversation and I was not particularly effective. After about 15 minutes we had not made progress toward a solution, and I had my eye on the clock. We were already going into overtime and I needed to get everybody out of the room. It was obvious this was not going to resolve quickly. Even on the "keep it" side there were *many* different opinions about what to do with the piece, and that side was becoming more and more polarized against the one person saying, "destroy it." People were getting frustrated and upset, and the prospect of a satisfying group closing was unraveling by the second. At this point, someone in the group stood up and proposed a vote for the "keep it" or "destroy it" alternatives. Before I could respond, a Native American from the MicMac tribe in eastern Canada stood up and faced me directly.

"Gerry, can I take over?" He asked. "I have an approach, and if you give me ten minutes by the clock, I'll have it solved." I had no idea what he had in mind, but I was more than glad to see what he could do. The discussion wasn't going anywhere useful.

He stepped up to the front of the room and first he asked, "Everybody's agreeing that we are ready to reach a resolution?" People nodded. He continued, "I have the solution if you're all willing to go along."

Everyone said, "Yeah, yeah, go ahead."

Then he turned to the man who wanted to destroy the artwork, and gesturing to him he spoke in a soft, deep voice that seemed utterly unconstrained by time.

"In my Native American tradition, when we have a group which is all on one side, and we have one person who is on another side, we would never have a vote to overrule him, because it's obvious that the majority will win, making him isolated.

We would never do that to someone.

So, the solution is we're going to turn over the responsibility for the decision to you—the one who's the isolated person. We're going to let you decide for all of us."

There was no mistaking that the words of the Native American were wholeheartedly genuine and sincere. He was really *completely* giving over the decision to this man.

I watched people's jaws hit the floor as the wave of shock moved through the room. But very quickly, I began to see certain people understand the wisdom in what the Native American had just done, and they relaxed a little.

The man who had been given responsibility to make the decision went through his own initial shock. At first there was a little glint in his eye which I'm guessing was his self-interest side, but then I could see a change taking place inside of him as well. His face went through several emotional swings, though I couldn't tell exactly what they meant. Pretty soon he stood up to speak.

"Well I think it's obvious we need to find a way that satisfies all of us," he said.

The tension in the room melted. Earlier, the man's argumentative tone had pitted him against the rest of the group, but as soon as the responsibility was completely in his hands, he changed his tone.

"My objection was that there wasn't a place where we could put the artwork," he said, "And I want to honor the spirit of what we all did together. Is there a place where we could put this piece of art where everybody would have access to it, and it would feel fair to all of us?"

Very quickly someone who had not been involved in the earlier discussion spoke up.

"I have a place," she said. "It's a big barn in the central U.S. where I could hang it. I also have a truck here; we could cut the piece in half to transport it, and once it's hanging up I can take a picture of it and send it to everybody, and anyone can drop by and visit it at any time."

Immediately, it was done. The shift was profound. The emotional ripple through the room was huge. You can tell the difference between people who are agreeing because they want an argument to be over, and people who are deeply satisfied. It was a wonderful moment. Everybody felt satisfied, including the man who had originally objected. The group was suddenly aligned and there was a powerful sense of completion.

I believe the reason this worked so well was because the group had such a strong relationship – this would not have worked unless that were so. The wisdom of the Native American in trusting responsibility with this one man made me imagine a culture in the business world in which that kind of approach was a common practice. With the proper intention and ground rules, what would that create? Surely such a profoundly unique way of working together could benefit organizational change.

My MicMac friend looked at his watch and said, "Seven minutes." [27]

Our Collaborative Nature

Some seeds grow only after passing through the digestive tract of a bird, which deposits the seed intact several miles away to avoid soil competition.

Geese fly in a "V" so they can all move faster.

Coral Reef and algae live together in a symbiotic relationship. Through photosynthesis, algae provide the coral with oxygen, essential to the survival of all living things. They are also the explanation behind the narrow temperature range that corals can live in. When the temperature of water rises as is happening now, coral polyps expel the algae, and consequently, the coral and algae both die.

Bumblebees and the flowers they pollinate have coevolved such that each is dependent on the other for survival. The flower may even develop specific characteristics for specific bee colonies, such as deep centers or certain bright color patterns that make it easier for the bees to find and pollinate them.

How can these examples inform organizational change?

Remember the saying "Go Slow to Go Fast" from earlier? There are no short-cuts to a facilitated conversation that builds shared understanding and ownership of any change or new project. And, as we pointed out in Chapter 4, this does not mean you engage in a "free-for-all" of idea-sharing. There is a skill set for structuring such a dialogue so it leads to a well-defined and relevant outcome.

Leaders who feel "it takes too much time" to help teams learn to build collaborative workplace cultures, should honestly evaluate how much time and productivity is lost in today's workplaces due to misunderstandings, confusion, and conflict when projects and initiatives are carried out via the traditional methods that "tell them what to do and expect it to be done." The research on this (Gallup from the Introduction) is quite clear on this subject.

We guarantee the payoff for implementing collaborative leadership more than outweighs the costs.

SUMMARY
Nature's Truth #5

In nature, everything is part of an interactive system.

In business, artificial boundaries must be dissolved to foster more interaction and cooperation, which produces more rapid adaptation.

1. We are tribal in nature: We work best when we organize ourselves in a relatively small clan with a shared purpose. Small, empowered teams can move faster!

2. The Industrial Age imposed unnatural adversarial relationships between boss and employee, and led to a loss of tribal wisdom in our workplaces. This is the root cause of today's lack of accountability and responsibility. As a leader, see your job as that of asking more questions to foster greater commitment and ownership.

3. We must recreate that wisdom by restoring the best of both worlds into our workplaces – efficiency and productivity along with shared ownership and accountability.

   • Cooperation inside, competition outside

   • Accountability and conflict – help people remember their natural tendency to be personally responsible, and watch how it reduces conflict

Making It Work! Small Changes for Building Collaborative Workplaces

If you keep in mind the mantra of ASK more often, the following best practices are rich territory for accelerating your efforts. To build more collaborative workplaces, implement a few of these best practices:

1) **Encourage collaboration.** Leaders need to take the time to set up shared goals that encourage people to reach across boundaries and cooperate in order to succeed. The new CEO of a successful pharmaceutical company noticed his company was severely silo'd. The SVP of manufacturing learned his area would have to ramp up production of a new product from reading an article in the Wall Street Journal. The SVP of Sales, who had been interviewed for the Wall Street article, was in an office three doors from the Manufacturing SVP. The CEO knew this needed to change, and created business strategy teams requiring the Senior VPs to meet regularly to figure out how to speed up the pipeline process. He deliberately structured the meetings to force interaction and collaboration on strategic issues.

2) **Reward teamwork.** People do what they are paid to do. A small manufacturing company revised its bonus structure so that 75% was determined by achievement of team goals. Revenue growth in the two years following the change was twice that of the prior two years, during an economic downturn.

3) **Bring people together.** Conduct forums in which people can meet and get to know one another across functional and geographical lines. The biggest benefit of the cross functional strategy teams in example #1 above was that the senior executives were forced to learn about each other's issues, needs, challenges and preferences for working. While there was great benefit from increased alignment, the CEO felt the biggest gains came from the increase in trust developed from more frequent meetings with more facilitated dialogue.

4) **Provide virtual collaboration tools.** Most organizations today are working, in some part, across several time zones. There are many tools for virtual and Web conferencing, and shared drives that encourage people to reach out to each other. But 88% of people report that they "multi-task" during these meetings, and are not fully attentive. We recently taught a course on reshaping the meeting culture as a lever for improving people's focus and time, and worked directly with this singular issue: The key to effective virtual collaboration is short meetings (30 minutes or less is ideal); few participants (5 or less is ideal); and a strong facilitator who creates and moderates a clear, focused GRPI (see Chapter 4), which was distributed in advance and remains visible during the meeting.

5) **Broaden SCRUM.** This powerful collaborative practice has emerged from the software development world, and is being used more widely as a framework for better project definition and time management. Originally borrowed from rugby, scrum was a method of beginning play in which the forwards of each team crouch side by side with locked arms —and the whole team tries to go the distance as a unit, passing the ball back and forth.

The main roles in scrum are the:

1. "ScrumMaster," who maintains the processes (typically in lieu of a project manager)

2. "Product Owner," who represents the stakeholders and/or the business

3. "Team," a cross-functional group of about 7 people who do the analysis, design, implementation, testing, etc.

The team defines a two-to-four-week goal (a sprint, specific length being decided by the team), bound by a potentially shippable product increment (for example, working and tested software). The set of features come from the Product Owner, who provides a priority set for the team. The team then determines how much of this they can commit to complete. *During a sprint, no one is allowed to change the sprint backlog*, which means the requirements are frozen for that sprint. After a sprint is completed, the team demonstrates the use of the software. Each day of the sprint, a project status meeting occurs. This is called a "daily scrum" or "the daily standup," in which:

- The meeting starts precisely on time.

- All are welcome, but only pigs* may speak.

- The meeting is time-boxed to 15 minutes.

- The meeting should happen at the same location and same time every day.

* Think about breakfast: The chicken participates - even contributes - at little or no pain. The pig commits fully at full cost. In the Agile world and in meetings in general, the chickens squawk a lot about what to do and who should do it. The pig does it – taking ownership to fully get it done. The team and the product owner are pigs. Anyone else who attends to observe is a chicken.

During the meeting, each team member answers three questions:

- What have you done since yesterday?

- What are you planning to do today?

- Do you have any problems preventing you from accomplishing your goal? (It is the role of the ScrumMaster to facilitate resolution of these impediments. Typically this should occur outside the context of the Daily Scrum so that it may stay under 15 minutes.[28]

What makes SCRUM work can be applied to any team or organization, especially when undergoing change:

1) Establish a clear, definable, *small chunk* goal.

2) Ensure a business sponsor has a stake in the outcome and scopes a clear agenda for the team.

3) Do "sprints" – 2-4 week efforts to prove you can get traction, during which you don't change scope.

4) Hold short, frequent meetings.

5) Define clear roles – recorder, timekeeper, facilitator.

6) Tie the effort to something a customer says they want.

Chapter 6: COMMUNICATION
Create a Steady Flow

Chapter 6 explores the importance of communication – which is always flowing regardless of whether it's being directed or managed effectively. We explore clear examples of what people want to know and how to ensure your leadership communication becomes a vehicle to create "pull to the right" – broader commitment that overcomes resistance or apathy to change.

Create a Steady Flow

Nature's Lesson #6:

In nature, communication flows
like water – endless and non-stop.

In business, information must flow more
naturally and leaders must help build bridges
and break down dams behind which meaning
and information are often stuck.

"What we've got here is a failure to communicate."

— Paul Newman & Strother Martin, from the 1967 film *Cool Hand Luke*

Whenever there is a storm surge or a flood, water exceeds its boundaries and leaks into places it's not supposed to. For human beings, organizational change is like a storm - and the flood is emotional. The "water overflows the banks" through rumors and guesses about what's happening – which usually are neither accurate nor positive. (Will my job be affected? What does this mean to *me*? Here we go *again...*)

Change invites insecurity to the party.

When insecurity accepts the invitation it leaks out as emotion. For people in organizations, that shows up as anger, frustration, cynicism or "checked out."

If there's one message we have for *any* leader during *any* change, it's COMMUNICATE MORE. There are two universal truths behind this advice:

1. **Change is "sold" with logic, but people commit through emotion.**

2. **People believe others see the world how they do.**

First, leaders place a high value on proof, logic, and convincing arguments over intangible characteristics such as intuition, empathy, and emotions. The latter is "soft stuff" and as such, is often uncomfortable and untrained territory for most leaders. Yet, it's how people commit – if I believe in it, if I believe in the leaders' commitment, it "ignites" something in me. That's an emotional journey, not a fact-based journey. (The word "emotion" is *not* synonymous with pep talks or people crying — more on this later.)

Second, a mistaken assumption we see leaders make is, "If *I* get it, they must too." When you have spent weeks or months constructing a breakthrough program or initiative, your communication comes from the point of view of having been immersed in it. But for them to understand it, to buy-in to it, will take them going through a process – just like you did.

This is reality. But sadly, leaders often ignore it – either because they think it's not important or because they don't know what to do about it. In almost every single change initiative we have seen, big or small, the typical form of communication during change is a short announcement with high-level platitudes and promises, followed by radio silence. The other most typical form is no communication at all. Most communications from leaders are blips on the screen in the day-in-the-life of an employee, rolling past with very little context, meaning, or perceived benefit. Sort of like the background announcement in the airport, "Attention: The TSA has determined a security level orange." If you travel frequently, you don't even hear it because the same message has been playing for nine years straight. (if you do hear it, you have no idea what you're supposed to DO about it.)

Further, information *itself* is a flood in our world. According to the Federal Reserve Bank of Dallas, each year enough new information goes into storage somewhere in the world to equal 37,000 Libraries of Congress. Talk about DATA OVERLOAD! Leaders who see a communication plan as a waste of time spend more time in disaster-recovery later from the rumor mill flood.

During an organizational change or new project/initiative, you need an intelligent process to cut through the overload and build meaning and commitment. With *any* new project or change, regardless of the size, people want to know the answer to five questions:

1) **Why are we doing this?**

2) **What's the plan? (high level vision AND details)**

3) **What's in it for me? (and do the people around me buy-in?)**

4) **What's expected of me? (how will my job change?)**

5) **What will leaders do to support it?**

Without a clearly structured communication plan to provide interactive dialogue between leaders and those who will be affected by – or implementing – the initiative or change, the chances of it achieving rapid buy-in and acceptance are very, very slim. If you issued the FYI memo, expect more WFC. (Who Freaking Cares?)

Bottom line: Communication builds motivation.

Why Is Communication During Change So Important?

John Kotter, the Harvard University professor and guru in organizational change, in his book "Leading Change" says it this way: "If the urgency rate isn't high, people don't listen carefully to information about the new vision. If the vision itself is too blurry or just a bad idea, selling poor goods becomes a tough job. But even when that's handled well, people still have difficulty because of the sheer magnitude of the task. Getting 100, 1,000 or 10,000 people to understand and accept a particular vision is an enormously challenging undertaking." (This was written in 1996.)

Dunbar's number sheds light on this situation.

Dunbar's number was first proposed by British anthropologist Robin Dunbar, who theorized a causal relationship between group size and group effectiveness. In his words "relative neo-cortex size limits group size, that is, the limit imposed by neocortical processing capacity is the number of individuals with whom a stable interpersonal relationship can be maintained." Stable relationships are defined as "an individual knows who each person is, and how each person relates to every other person."

A fancy way of saying that in organizations, we are only as smart as our relationships.

No precise value has been proven for Dunbar's number, but a commonly cited approximation is 150 people.

If Dunbar is right (our experience suggests that he is), when an organization has exceeded about 150 people, it's difficult to foster easy connectivity. That has a *tremendous impact* on productivity and effectiveness. You simply can't maintain a sense of shared meaning and purpose within a large group (at least not without a robust and conscious communication plan). And we all know that shared purpose is what leads to a "movement" – the Arlo Guthrie definition of making something good happen, from the famous song *Alice's Restaurant*.

If vision is the destination, communication is the lubricant that accelerates aligned movement toward it. Kotter reports in his research that communication during change is typically under-done by a factor of at least 10 times what's needed; very often the factor is more like 100x.

This is similar to the process of building brand recognition of a product or company – it takes patience, time, repetition, consistency; and you have to *deliver on the promise.*

Remember the 2009 Gallup research from the Introduction? Approximately 2 out of every 3 workers (across small and large companies) are either "biding their time" or "actively disengaged" at work? The level of disconnected people in organizations is unprecedented across our business world today – largely because there is very little done to create a workplace culture that links people's activity to a consistent, meaningful purpose.

Communication during change is not a small "nice-to-have." As a leader, your #1 job is to make effort to cut through the noise, the cynicism, the craziness, the overload… and make sense to people.

The Impact of Too Little Communication

We aren't saying communication isn't happening already. Communication is like a river – it's a constant flow and exchange of ideas, information, and gossip going around your team, department, or company all the time. That's what people DO.

As a leader, you may understand a thing or two about communicating during change: You got the memo, right? But during change, *how* you handle communication with employees must also change. Remember that communication is always flowing. During change, there is often a "parting of the river" between leaders and employees. It may look like the "same" water but there are separate streams moving in different directions. The leader's job is to converge the streams into one river. There are specific methods for doing so that have a positive impact on people's *actions.* An email won't do it. Think dialogue, not monologue.

People want a credible story for how the new team, initiative, or merger is a bridge to something *better.* They want confidence that if they undertake personal sacrifice in the short term, it will lead to them to being able to personally grow, learn or take more pride in their work. That's what your employees care about. Profitability is YOUR measuring stick – you can and should *measure* by it, but it doesn't *motivate* your people.

Most of all, your people want to talk with their manager to find out what it means for them personally, and to trust and restore confidence in the future.

But monologue speeches are common, such as: "Our goal is to become the truly transnational firm at the conjunction of the converging communication/information industries to achieve both a boundaryless organization and a paradigm shift strategy." (a real quote from a famous leader)

"These are very hard times for our company. We must make hard decisions, prioritize carefully, and guard ourselves against wasteful spending wherever possible. Our vision is to relentlessly cut costs." (An actual vision statement from a large company we worked with; be sure you don't deliver that one after public knowledge that executives took sizable bonuses.)

Do either of these stories get your juices flowing and ready to jump all over this new opportunity? How many hours do you think an executive or marketing team spent crafting these words? Sadly, nobody outside the 2-3 people who wrote them has any idea what they mean, knows what to do about them, or honestly cares a whit.

Rule #1 of communication: If your audience isn't personally invested in and able to act on what you're saying, your message will sound just like the adults in the classic Charlie Brown cartoons: "Wa *wa* wa *wa* wa wa."

Mark is a Navy pilot who flew numerous combat missions during Desert Storm and other high-risk missions. Recently Mark and Lisa were having lunch, and he was sharing stories from the cockpit. In Mark's world, communication practices are life-and-death, literally. They are taken very seriously. Mark's stories can provide some clues for leaders:....

Mark's Story

" Especially during take-off, too much information too soon is overload. So, I'm sitting in the cockpit and my co-pilot is saying,"These guys are going to be on deck before we even start taxiing." "There's a flock of birds out there."

"Is that relevant to me right now?"

As the pilot in command, I would often announce, "Sanitize the cockpit." This means "If I don't need to know it, don't give it to me." Do NOT say anything that isn't absolutely necessary to the safety of the flight.

When you take off from an aircraft carrier at night, especially during bad weather, it's like getting in your car and starting down a lonely country road with no lights – and you floor it. Then someone throws a blanket over your windshield. Except instead of 0-60 in six seconds, we go from 0-120 knots in 3 seconds. As the pilot, you are totally focused on your instruments, and the minute details of the take-off.

On an aircraft carrier, each plane has a unique catapult setting – once in awhile the setting would be too low for that aircraft or there would be a malfunction, which means you don't get enough power to stay airborne. When this happens, the plane will drop right into the water.

So, immediately following a particular take-off, — we had just left the flight deck: The most crucial moments following a cat shot — my co-pilot says "Oh shit!" Loudly.

I have one hand on the ejection handle and one hand on the flight controls, and I'm about to eject — which means you lose a $50 million dollar aircraft (an S-3 Viking) and go into the water — and now you have a 19 ton aircraft bearing down on your face...IF you survive the ejection. That's the last thing you want to have happen. Ending up in the ocean, tangled in parachute shrouds and fabric, disoriented, likely injured from the ejection and scared to death as a 97,000 ton aircraft carrier bears down on you...in the dark. That has a tendency to ruin your entire day.

I look over at my co-pilot and ask "What's Up?"

"My map light just burned out," he replies.

Once I got the airplane up to our assigned altitude and in a straight and level configuration, there was somewhat of a debrief about how to communicate during lift-off and what a "sanitized cockpit" means. It went something like "Don't you EVER tell me that your map light has burned out again during the takeoff evolution!!!" Only it was a accompanied by me pounding him in the helmet with my kneeboard.

You put human beings in stressful situations and their human-ness is going to come through. What the navy hopes, and what you hope, is all the intense training overrides the human-ness, and when bad things start happening, your training takes over.

There's no substitute for excellent training, sound judgment and communication between people in a cockpit when it comes to flying an aircraft and keeping it as safe as possible.

It's great to have an extra person in the cockpit – the jets today are very sophisticated. The last aircraft I flew was rated for 2.5 human beings (how the navy is able to count ½ a person is beyond me). This rating is intended to convey the number of "actual human beings" it takes to maximize the potential of the jet. Yet, often I was the only person in the jet. You put little old me in there and let me get overwhelmed, and you are never maximizing the full potential of the jet – optimizing how fast it can turn, how well it can track missiles — one pilot can't assimilate it all.

That's why, in this particular aircraft, we have one person navigating and communicating and one person driving the jet around.

We fly a flight pattern to land on a carrier – which is a very small target – and my only attention is keeping the green ball (affectionately referred to by naval aviators as the "meat ball") in the cross-hairs off to left side of ship. That's what I'm concentrating on. If there is anything outside that field of vision on the flight deck, I probably won't see it. So the co-pilot is watching the flight deck, watching the back of the ship, and he might call "foul deck" – should someone drive a piece of equipment out into the landing area or a person accidentally strolls out into the landing area...It's possible, with all I'm engaged in and concentrating on, I might now see that – the co-pilot helps spot the dangers I might not see.

It's always good to have redundancy.

Amidst the flood of change being cascaded through every organization, Too Much Information guarantees Too Little Meaning. When leaders don't translate their message into *personal terms* and link to a common purpose and values, they see the flood of serial change initiatives creating a "Workplace A.D.D." – a frenetic energy and lack of clear focus in which people tune out, disengage, and stop taking it in – simply as a way to survive.

Remember in Chapter 2 on vision, when our client said to his Quality organization "Are we going to fix the roof or keep emptying the bucket?"? His people were engaged both by the motivation to create a better result, and the embarrassment of past failure. It was *personal.*

After John Kennedy pledged America would get a man to the moon and back to earth safely by the end of that decade, the scientists at NASA literally ran to their desks to help make that happen. A lot of their motivation was about "beating Russia." (Evoking a little competitive drive helps too.) What did it mean to them personally? The opportunity to create a lasting legacy and create new, unimagined benefits for society many years beyond the moon-walk program. The best leaders made sure they kept this message visible, especially when the going got difficult (which it always does).

Bob is a recent client of Gerry's who is a minister of a church working in one of the poorest communities in the U.S. Gerry was consulting with him and discussing the importance of enough communication during change. Bob explained how for the first year they were working together, he started every meeting by having someone on his team read the vision statement, and explain what it meant to them. "We are a diverse community of people who are inspired and empowered to make the community better for generations to come." After a year, he said it was amazing to see and hear how aligned his team had become. These people aren't sophisticated or trained in leadership, but they understand why they are there, and remembering it at each meeting makes sure.

Creating an emotionally compelling message is the foundation of extraordinary effort and results. Simpler is better.

Pull To the Right

If change is emotional, the goal of communication during change is to dispel negative emotions of fear and create positive emotions: hope, anticipation, excitement.

If you have ever tried to talk someone out of their fear through logic, you have your answer about why most leadership communication doesn't work. And, too much of the time, the job of communicating is left to managers who are most comfortable in routine fact-based communications.

Adding a compelling reason for change does not mean being insincere to who you are, building a touchy-feely process, or a bunch of motivational rah-rah sessions (those often make things worse). It does mean ensuring that you've covered the need for people to understand WHY in a way that's credible, and the answer is something they care about. We work with a lot of engineers (in fact, Gerry was trained as one). Engineers need facts and proof for change – you can't short-change that. And, they are often stubborn about change, thus the steady stream of re-orgs

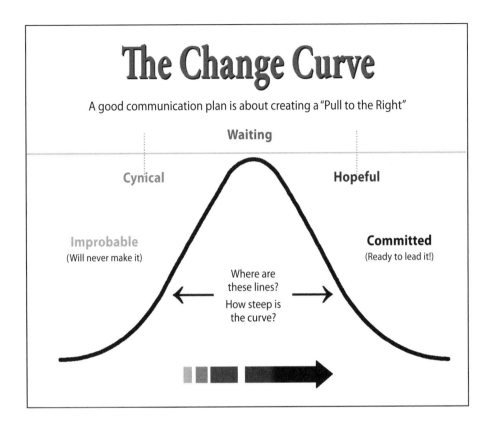

The Change Curve

A good communication plan is about creating a "Pull to the Right"

Waiting

Cynical   Hopeful

Improbable   **Committed**
(Will never make it)   (Ready to lead it!)

Where are
these lines?
⟵   How steep is   ⟶
the curve?

Fostering a pull to the right takes persistence, patience, and perseverance. Getting people excited about an unknown future is harder than continuing on a trajectory of a known past.

In our pharmaceutical example, the Quality leader engaged us to train a cadre of internal quality experts in how to build buy-in and commitment during change (which he followed up with active mentoring). The team was given the responsibility for co-developing the plan that would save the company from financial ruin. They built the high-level plan, then translated it into a detailed story that explained in simple and compelling language the vision for the remedy, the plan to get there, and what was in it for all the employees who would be part of the solution. After months of creating alignment among the core group, they took their story on the road to multiple manufacturing sites around the globe. There, they enrolled people through discussion forums in which people could explore how the global plan would adapt to their local situation. In every case those forums would start out with a high degree of skepticism. Next, resistance and doubt. Later, interest. After enough consistent interaction on the need for change, people moved toward commitment and engagement.

When you strike the right balance of urgency (what happens if we don't change?) and vision (an exciting future that are we moving toward) you tap into people's personal motivation and important influential relationships around them, which create *collective* urgency for the change. In turn, that drives a strong pull toward commitment.

What's YOUR Commitment-pull Currently?

- Are the people on your team or in your organization showing high energy and excitement about the initiatives or projects you are undertaking, or is there a sense of confusion, lackluster commitment, or cynicism?

- Do the key influencers within the teams believe in your vision?

- Are important deadlines being easily met or plagued by excuses?

- Do projects regularly meet established budgets, or do scope-creep and unexpected curve balls continually increase their expense?

- If an outsider asked 15 randomly selected members of your team to state the vision of their leader and rate how inspired they are by it on a scale of 1-10 – would the answers come back using the same words? Would the average be close to 10?

Where do we stand with Bill, Dan, and Charles? Given the size and scope of the initiative they were undertaking, communication was a crucial element. But the span across so many divisions and geographies made it challenging to strike a balance between providing adequate communication for everyone that was not "generic," and which was also tailored to what each person and team needed to know. Town hall meetings had good attendance, some people felt the messages were too broad; others felt they were redundant. The team opted for a simple FAQ of the basics, and a regular blog-style update on the progress of the initiative. Further, they decided to invite the Initiative sponsors to key team meetings, to foster informal "roll up your sleeves" dialogue. We also helped them create a Survey Monkey tool to pinpoint the cultural problem areas of un-discussed habits and mindsets hindering the change process across the business. In such a large initiative, it helps to develop a theme for each quarter, stating clear communication goals and processes.

Here is an excerpted sample of their communication plan:

Vehicle	Frequency	Responsible	What Is It	Participants	Purpose
1. Team meetings	Monthly and/ or after Town Hall meetings	Owner: Team Managers Support: Sponsors	Informal face-to-face, highly interactive meeting Get feedback/ key comments	Initiative Stakeholders with Sponsor attendance	Address concerns and questions regarding _____ goals, plans, progress. Help teams understand their role in supporting _____.
2. Blog, SharePoint	On-going	Owner: TBD Support: Odyssey core and extended team members, sponsors	Feed site with regular updates, wins/ success stories. Use video/ other multi-media forms of communication that people can access at anytime.	GPDG, GBG	Communicate _____ goals, plans, & progress. Messages would tie to initiative updates, significant wins, announcements, team accomplishments. Address Q&A based on culture survey and Town Hall meetings.

Newton's Laws of Motion and Communication

Newton's Laws of Motion can help us further illustrate why it's difficult to create a "pull to the right" toward collective commitment to something new.

Law #1: Every object in a state of uniform motion tends to remain in that state of motion unless an external force is applied to it.

As stated earlier, people are creatures of habit. We tend to stay on the path of least resistance until we are sufficiently dissatisfied with the status quo OR a compelling new opportunity presents itself. During change, a leader is the "external force," but often doesn't provide enough to overcome inertia. The change is announced, but the energy and momentum remain on the old trajectory.

Further, most change initiatives don't have a positive force toward something meaningful, clear, or compelling to people. Change efforts today are mostly status quo dressed-up in a change costume; in people's minds they are lumped into the category of "cut costs and do more with less." The result is often, "I'll try to play the game, but quarterly earnings isn't a reason to greatly inconvenience myself; it just puts money in someone *else's* pocket. " Cynicism grows as a result.

A common spiral you want to avoid:

GOAL: Increase profits
  OUTSIDE: Increasing competitive pressure and speed →
    YOU RESPOND: Cost cuts and "lean" the organization
      NOW YOU HAVE: Fewer people working harder and faster →
        WHICH MEANS: Less time and resources to truly innovate →
          GOOD PEOPLE: Burn out, disengage, leave →
          DECREASED productivity and higher talent costs →
            REALITY: Squeeze on profits
              Begin cycle again

Human beings have free will and complex motives. Simple carrot-and-stick motivators rarely produce real change.

Second, remember the leaky emotion problem?

If change raises insecurities for people, a good communication process can help them to buy-in; process their fears; possibly grieve for lost colleagues; and see themselves doing things differently to support the new way. Messages to "pump up the numbers" or "innovate" have no relevance in their world. They don't provide adequate force to step off their current path.

One of the most critical initiatives in every company today should be winning trust within the crucial connection between executives and employees, and helping them translate high-level platitudes into relevant information at the project team and department level.

And do that 100X more than you think is necessary.

Law #2: Force = *Mass* x *Acceleration (F = ma)*. Large, heavy, dense objects require more force to move faster.

How do you get an airplane off the ground versus a hang-glider?

Gerry was recently traveling to the northeast coast, and his original flight was cancelled due to weather. They rebooked him through another city on a regional jet – as a result that flight was now double its original passenger load. After everyone boarded the flight and the doors were closed, the captain came on and said, "Ladies and Gentlemen, we just learned that Charleston's long runway is closed. Given the added weight of our plane, we will be unable to take off on the short runway. We need to ask several people to volunteer to get off the plane in order to take off." What followed was a very long process to deplane 15 people and their luggage, by which time Gerry and several other passengers missed their connections to their destination.

Business improvement initiatives are commonly aborted due to runway length. Lift-off requires speed and thrust to overcome drag (weight). You often don't discover this problem until you are already underway. You've made the decision to proceed and discover you have to backtrack, take extra time to unload baggage (resources that aren't available) and scale the change to something you *can* implement. Meanwhile, your competitor may beat you in the market by executing a series of smaller take-offs faster.

Successfully overcoming Law #2 is about optimizing for take-off on a short runway: Scoping projects to the smallest scale that can get airborne quickly, and communicating smaller successes.

When the change is BIG naturally and by design (like a merger), it requires a LOT of new behaviors by a LOT of people. Know ahead of time it's going to be a very LONG runway, and you'll need a lot of fuel (communication and attention from sponsors) to achieve lift-off. A primary reason most mergers fail is adequate work to integrate the two organizations effectively was never done: heavy plane, short runway.

Never underestimate the power of gravity.

Law #3: For every action there is an equal and opposite reaction.

The natural instinct of a person facing "external change" is fight or flight, not open arms. In the world of business, this shows up as backlash, pushback and resistance (as demonstrated in the Gallup data showing 2/3 of the workforce is disengaged or worse).

Alignment is achieved by managing opposition reactions effectively and persistently enough to get the flywheel moving in the new direction.

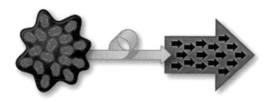

There are three elements of working with this law of motion:

First, strong, persistent, and patient leadership communication that aligns with negative energy (early on) is the best method to transform it. Aikido is the martial art of using someone's offensive energy in a way that diffuses it, rather than escalates it. There are volumes written on this principle, but it is simply the art of seeking to understand the resistance and align with it, rather than immediately posturing in opposition to it.

Second, create executive alignment at the top. Too many leaders see the hard work of creating cross-functional alignment with their peers, with its inherent trade-offs and conflicts, as soft, unnecessary or a distraction. They try to muscle through resistance based on their own commitment. This creates more resistance, and results in more widespread dissatisfaction, confusion and apathy. It's important for a sponsoring executive to meet 1:1 with his peers to get their concerns out on the table and begin to educate them about the importance of the initiative or project.

A classic example can be found in Business Process Simplification and Lean Initiatives. Lean is the new cool thing in most organizations. It has a simple goal: Remove waste in your processes. It is commonly sponsored by the IT organization, who partner with process experts from HR or Learning. These groups are enthusiastic, passionate and effective at process design. Often, their solutions are elegant, BIG, and don't involve key resistors in their design. Pretty soon, they run into the inevitable pushback from the field – e.g., marketing, sales, research: "We don't want to do it *that* way. We've always done it *this* way." If the IT and HR executives have not sufficiently built buy-in with their peers in the boardroom, alignment and adoption don't occur down the chain. Their initiatives are plagued by apathy or active resistance from people who don't want to change – and whose leaders aren't telling them they have to.

Third, people often shield leaders from the truth and don't *provide* respectful pushback: resistance also strengthens (think of weight training). Many offer a polite "head-nod" to a leader's ideas, but inside they are saying "Here we go again. New flavor of the month!" Then everyone goes back to their offices and does what they've always done. This game is being played out over and over, eroding trust between the very groups who need to be in truthful dialogue that forges alignment. Communicating up the chain is as important as communicating down.

Leaders who see building alignment as their #1 job during change – and invest time and energy in it – move faster to overcome Law #3.

Communicate, communicate, communicate.

Say it 100 times more than you think is necessary and get into the flow in which true change can occur.

SUMMARY
Nature's Truth #6

In nature, communication flows like water – endless and non-stop.

In business, information must flow more naturally and leaders must help build bridges and break down dams behind which meaning and information are often stuck.

Commitment is an emotional process, but change is often "sold" as a logical process.

Communication is always happening. During change, leaders need to manage it to overcome negativity and create positive "pull" toward commitment.

Frequent, clear communication is how you overcome the natural tendency to resist change. It takes 10-100 times more than you think it will.

Three laws of motion – inertia, gravity, and resistance – offer clues about the role of leadership communication during change.

Making It Work! Small Changes for Effective Communication during Change

1. **Use more emotion and personal information.**
   What people need to hear is what's in this for them, and why you leaders care about that. This must be more emotional than factual. "Why I'm excited about this and what my stake in it is..." You've spent a long time getting to this place; you have to guide people through a similar journey.

2. **Foster more alignment.** One of the most important elements of leadership communication is the willingness and time of leaders to actively work with their peers in other parts of the organization to facilitate broader alignment of the vision and goals. This results in several leaders telling a common story.

3. **Communicate in small, interactive groups.** We often design and teach our clients to conduct "culture forums" in which people are invited to explore "how can we be the very best we can be?" in a very specific, tangible way. This is a more organized venue to discuss the unquestioned, the untouchable and the un-discussed. Done well, this creates a shared sense of meaning, identity and purpose —and releases tremendous energy and commitment.

4. **Walk the Talk.** During change, communication must be managed in two basic, equally important forms:

   a) What You Do

   Leaders need to be seen visibly aligning resources, priorities, and decisions to actively support the change.

The most successful change initiatives spend a lot of time creating results, before they spend time creating communication programs that talk about the great plans.

This seems counterintuitive to many leaders, but you can trust us – the right order is "walk before you talk."

b) What You Say

This is not just what you say but how you say it - including your tone, enthusiasm and clarity.

Similar to branding in the marketing world, a common story and communication process that coordinates across business units is a crucial step for building trust, credibility, understanding, and alignment – and breaking down boundaries.

There are five questions people want to know the answer to during change:

1. **Why are we doing this? (what's the opportunity)**

2. **What happens if we don't (creates a sense of urgency and importance)**

3. **What does the change look like or mean? (vision)**

4. **What's in it for me? (and what's expected of me)**

5. **What will leaders do to support it (includes changes in resources and priorities)**

– Section Three –
Evolve through Learning
(Chapters 7-9)

The third lesson from nature is that growth IS change: It's called evolution. In business, leaders must create a system for stimulating a balance of stability and evolution. It takes patience and persistence to overcome the tendency to become comfortable and complacent. The greater the success and the bigger the size, the more this is true. Leaders must foster a continuous process of feedback and small changes – but also not expect everything to be different overnight. We call this balance "being adaptable."

In chapter 8, after learning a new way of thinking about their parent company, one leadership team secured a $450M investment for their business a year later. Stories like Louis' transformation of his software company in Chapter 9, tell us that small change is real, and evolution is possible.

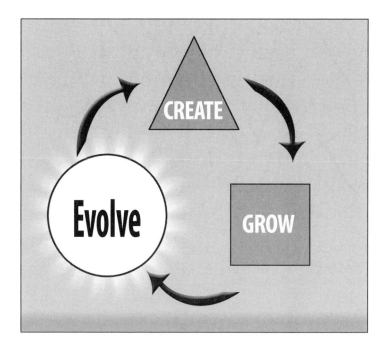

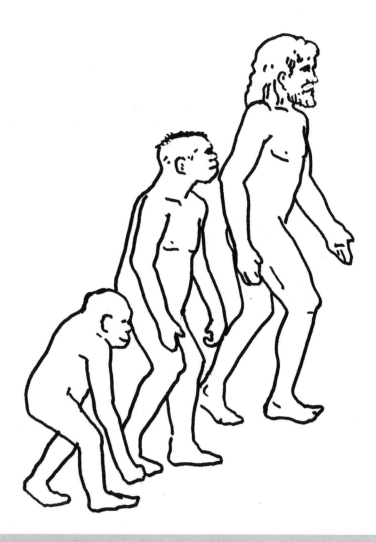

Chapter 7: LEARN
Avoid Extinction by Adapting

In Chapter 7, we explore learning as nature's way of being adaptable, especially in fast-changing and extreme conditions. We offer ideas for what you can do to create a business culture that reflects learning as its core principle, and embed learning in whatever you do.

Avoid Extinction by Adapting

Nature's Truth #7:

Nature uses learning to avoid extinction.

In business, building a learning culture is the remedy to support an environment of sustainable growth.

"Would you like a formula for success? It's quite simple. Double your rate of failure. Go ahead and make mistakes. Make all you can. Remember that's where you'll find success. On the far side."

— Thomas J. Watson, founder, IBM

Nature keeps things pretty simple.

Those who adapt survive – and sometimes thrive.

Those who don't, become extinct.

Remember 70-75% of all organizational change efforts fail to produce the desired result. This poor success rate of adapting does not bode well for the survival of many companies today – let alone being the most fit to compete. Look to your own experience for evidence: How many projects have you led in the past 5 years

– personally and professionally – that represent a significant change for yourself and those around you?

How many of those would you call an unqualified, raving success?

If you said "all of them" – please call us. Our clients would like to meet you and we want to model your success.

But if you're like most people, "the results were mixed" – and at least one or two were an outright failure. If you dig deeper into the reasons, usually you will say that the difference was rarely about available knowledge, resources, or technology. There is no shortage of approaches for implementing great ideas, theoretically. Everyone has *access* to a sophisticated pool of knowledge and information about how to effectively change and adapt.

If the methods to adapt and change are well known and resources are available to make them work, why don't they *work*?

First, organizations are set up and structured to create a stable, consistent operation, versus a dynamic system that can learn and adapt. Karl Popper, the great 20th century science philosopher illustrates the importance of doing both when he said: "We must plan for freedom and not only for security, if for no other reason than only freedom can make security secure."

Second, most organizations have a significant hierarchical mentality, in which leaders and managers are not aware of the challenges and ideas of those who implement change.

Most of us have heard of the company, Roto-Rooter. In April 2010, President and COO Rick Arquilla posed as an everyday plumber in the reality show "Undercover Boss" to learn about his company and the people who worked in it.

The experience was transformational for him. By posing as an everyday worker, he got an up-close view of how difficult the work was. He learned details of stories from people who were working really hard to make a good name for his company – giving their best. Through hearing their stories, he learned very personal lessons about himself: that he had not healed his relationship with his alcoholic father; that his people were deeply worried about outsourcing their jobs overseas; and that he wanted to leave a legacy of a great company by giving back. These truths moved him to tears, literally. Later, he commented that to see the culture of an organization through the eyes of your own people is very powerful and humbling.

There is little chance Rick would have heard these stories or discovered these truths if he had shown up at the sites as the "real boss." People would have rolled out the red carpet and put their best face on. Because employees thought he was one of them, he was able to learn the truth about what they really thought and cared about. And he didn't stop with awareness: he made decisions that impacted those employees lives' in profound ways. This included helping an autistic child whose mother worked long hours in his dispatch organization; helping another employee learn to inspire others by telling his journey through alcohol recovery; purchasing a 15-passenger van for a supervisor who coached basketball after work 4 nights per week. These may have been relatively small changes in Rick's world, but they fostered tremendous trust and connection between he and his employees.

Remember the Harvard study on "leadership" where they found that the two qualities most common among authentic leaders were self-awareness and commitment to ongoing learning? Rick Arquilla stepped out of his comfort zone and got a big dose of both.

In nature, survival of the fittest is the rule: Organisms that evolve or adapt to their environment are the ones that prosper. In nature, evolution is a natural process of ongoing learning. For all the reasons we have explored in earlier chapters about the "organizational entity" having been separated from an awareness of its system, learning is a conscious activity leaders must embed – based on two major principles from nature:

- **Feedback - any biological system without a "feedback loop" will eventually become extinct. Finding a method to give your people more frequent and direct contact with the outside world (customers, vendors, competitors) will benefit any team or organization, no matter the size.**

- **Autonomy – In nature, choice and consequences are contained within the entity: a tree that doesn't adapt, dies. As we described** in Chapter 5, industrial age management practices have interrupted this natural cycle in human societies: Managers set the goals and hand them off to the employee to achieve. Tapping into people's innate motivation and drive to learn is not seen as relevant to the bottom line. But the predominance of external motivation is backfiring. In his book *"Drive: The Surprising Truth About What Motivates Us"* (c 2009, The Penguin Group) Daniel Pink relates research studies that show, once an individual has met "basic survival needs," traditional carrot-and-stick incentives produce the *exact opposite* of their intended aims. That is, if you pay people to perform, you will reliably see diminished performance.

When you create an environment in which learning is the central aim, you ignite the natural process in which sustainable, rapid adaptability happen. People become excited and commit beyond your wildest imagination. Their collective energy creates surprising results that managers could never have planned for (as we learned in Rick Arquilla's story, a manager or executive cannot easily gain full access of what it's like to work with the customers, products/services, systems, and structure within your company).

We have identified two important activities for embedding learning in a culture in a way that allows people to adapt and thrive:

(1) Broaden Your Perspective (Detect the Need for Change)

Imagine you are sitting on the banks of the Mississippi River delta near New Orleans. You turn to your child and say, "This is the Mississippi River." Is this an accurate statement? Yes. You are both looking at the Mississippi River. Is it a complete one? No. Because, unless you are several thousand miles above earth, you aren't aware there is someone else 1,000 miles upstream having the exact same conversation with their child. And, their view is accurate too.

This seems obvious when talking about known geography, but leaders often miss the importance of this perspective and truth. There are many factors outside of our awareness that cause the condition of the downstream part of the "river" called "results." Detecting threats and opportunities is about widening your lens and seeing a bigger landscape – and finding ways to see parts of the river that are not familiar to you. Identifying strengths and minimizing weaknesses - the process of natural selection in nature – requires holding a broader perspective than what is or is not working in this moment.

Adaptive leaders pay attention to a broad range of signals outside their immediate environment. They seek people and perspectives that are different from their own. The signals they attend to are not what they are most familiar with or have been trained to attend to. They don't use their financial results as a way to self-congratulate or become preoccupied with how to replicate that same success. They undertake a process to keep learning, to ensure they are tuned into what is changing in the environment that matters to their business, so they will know how to respond.

And, they help their employees do the same. The world of an average employee is a small corner of the business – producing one piece of a product or service with little insight into how the business operates. The leaders' vision, strategy or financial goals are an abstract concept. In most companies, unless you are in sales or customer service, you have little insight into the needs of the marketplace or customers your efforts serve. The people who are closest to the marketplace and customers are often not encouraged or rewarded to detect opportunities that could improve the business, because they are not empowered to make decisions to respond. As we pointed out earlier, leadership strategy, decision making, and employee actions are typically disconnected from one another in today's business world.

Leaders who invest time to visibly link the front line employees' daily activities, projects and decisions to the company's survival *or* to something with personal meaning, find that learning and adaptability happens more naturally than by initiating a lot of formal change initiatives, and trying to convince employees that they are a good idea.

One of our clients is the CEO of a small, family-owned construction company run by a brother-and-sister team. Both partners share a strong belief in creating a values-driven workplace, but the organization was not seeing productivity at the levels necessary to sustain profitable performance. In construction, labor is the most significant variable in meeting the bid, and more cost pressure is being put on contractors in the current economy. It was important for the partners to articulate, and put into writing, a clear vision and values that tell everyone how they are different: their belief and experience that customers would be willing to pay a little more for the peace of mind and professionalism exhibited by a company that really cares about quality.

But the most important change they have made was a process to identify strengths and weaknesses in each field employee; to educate field supervisors about why field productivity is so important, and clarify what behaviors each person can DO to improve it. This has resulted in greater consistency and productivity numbers are increasing as a result, even though very little has changed about how jobs are bid. Every month, the supervisors come together and discuss the subject of how important it is to do a high-quality, professional job – and to ensure that each person who represents this contractor knows the importance of showing up with the same standard of professionalism.

The more leaders help *other* people to see things differently, the less time they need to spend figuring out how to create buy-in to change. Creating buy-in is like digging out of a hole: You will not be able to raise everyone higher until everyone has climbed out of the hole and are standing at ground zero.

Why? Fear is a survival mechanism for every species. The rose has thorns. The tiger has claws and teeth. When leaders make decisions regarding change (e.g., another re-org) without input from, or a relationship with, the people being impacted, people's fight or flight response is triggered. External change is perceived as a *personal* threat or loss. To make things worse, leaders are often afraid of people's fear, seeing it as emotional territory to be avoided and inappropriate in business. But when people are imagining the worst: "I'll lose my job…I'll lose the respect of my employees/peers if I commit… This will never really work anyway..." their cynicism grows and they shut down – taking their creativity and productivity with them.

When you name the fear and discuss it, it's like shining a flashlight under your child's bed so they can see the boogeyman doesn't live there. Especially when you don't *have* the answers or you cannot fix the situation to make it "OK" for everyone, allowing people to be heard is a tremendously powerful small change any leader can do to create more cooperation and trust.

Another important action leaders can take to broaden perspective during change is by repetition of the subject we've talked about throughout this book: Vision. Every person has a burning desire to fulfill a purpose encoded in them, right beside their fear-gene. (Some have forgotten it or lost it, but *everyone* has it.) A leader with vision sends the message: "I'm willing to face down the bullies who would see us fail and the obstacles that will challenge us, in service of building something great." When you come from this place, you ignite willingness on the part of a team or organization to tune in and detect opportunities or obstacles, and to endure mistakes, in order to learn.

Broadening perspective is all about getting more people's "radar" onto:

- **Competitors (threats) who could beat you in the race;**

- **Customers (opportunities) who can help you turn the corner faster and gain a lap on your competitors;**

- **Building on clear strengths and minimizing weaknesses (improving natural selection)**

(2) Respond Fast

Predicting the future accurately in the face of rapid competitive forces is much harder these days.

Organizations must increase their ability to move *faster* and adapt more quickly to offset the increasing uncertainty of prediction.

Here's the catch:

Human beings talk themselves into staying in their comfort zone even when that choice puts their life or future at risk. When resources are dwindling due to drought or over-population (or competitors are outpacing you) this is sign of imbalance and signals the need for change. The appropriate response is movement – toward something *different*.

Far too many organizational leaders act like Captain Edward John Smith of the Titanic: ignoring the warning signs of icebergs and assuming they will see anything big enough to sink the ship in time. This often happens when leaders are rewarded based on a myopic, small view: the growth of earnings through quarterly profits. Taking time to develop a strategic ability to adapt is often seen as time-consuming and pitted against short-term results.

Now seems a good time to mention the Black Swan Theory.

"Black swan" was a common expression in 16th century London to describe impossibility, deriving from the old world presumption that all swans must be white because all historical records of swans reported that they had white feathers. When explorer Willem de Vlamingh led an expedition in1697 that discovered black swans, the term became popular to describe a perceived impossibility may later be found to exist.

The Black Swan Theory was developed by Nassim Nicholas Taleb to explain (1) the disproportionate role of high-impact, hard-to-predict, and rare events that are beyond the realm of normal expectations in history, science, and technology (he cites the internet, the personal computer, World War I, and 9-11-2000) and (2) the psychological biases that make people individually and collectively blind to uncertainty and unaware of the role of the rare event.

What Taleb calls a Black Swan is an event with three attributes. First, it is an outlier, as it lies outside the realm of regular expectations. Nothing in the past can convincingly point to its possibility. Second, it carries an extreme impact. Third, in spite of its outlier status, human nature makes us concoct explanations for its occurrence after the fact, making it explainable and predictable. Taleb points out that a small number of Black Swans explains almost everything in our world, from the success of ideas and religions, to the dynamics of historical events, to elements of our own personal lives.

The main idea in Taleb's book is for us not to attempt to predict Black Swan Events, but to build robust abilities to respond to negative impacts, and the ability to exploit positive ones. Taleb further states that a Black Swan Event depends on the observer. What may be a Black Swan surprise for a turkey is not a Black Swan surprise for its butcher—hence the objective should be to "avoid being the turkey" by identifying areas of vulnerability in order to "turn the Black Swans white".

Black Swan Theory reminds us that predicting the future is not nature's plan. As we will explore in the remainder of this chapter, there are models of evolution that point to how we can create a collective ability to respond quickly, and capitalize on your own Black Swans.

In nature (and often in business too) evolution and extinction are not rapid processes. In the 100 generations of human evolution since the Roman Empire, there have been relatively minute adaptations in human beings. Yet the changes in the human environment during that time have been enormous (diet, habitation, working conditions, chemicals, pollution of air and water). Sometimes populations undergo a phenomenon called additive genetic variation – a kind of turbocharged natural selection in which a rapid environmental change may cause bursts of rapid changes in the entity.

Bottom line, if the outside changes more rapidly than the inside is adapting, you die. The same can be said of many legacy corporations with cultures that are insular and unfriendly to change.

One of the biggest threats leaders face in today's business climate is that of waiting for the right time and *changing too slowly*. Evolutionary science is providing clues about how leaders can help their organizations learn to adapt more quickly.

An example of a system in nature that *has* learned to evolve quickly is bacteria. A quirk of bacteria is the root cause of antibiotic resistance: horizontal transfer. Most organisms evolve through genetic mutation: "Small accidents" in the genetic code are passed from parent to offspring; if they are advantageous they spread. But in bacteria, new gene variants are passed back and forth directly through DNA.

They don't even have to be closely related to share DNA. (There are particular implications for organizational culture about this, which we will explore later.)

Another example of rapid adaptability is in the emerging science of Complex Adaptive Systems (CAS). CAS refers to a dynamic network of many agents (cells, species, individuals, firms, nations) acting in parallel, constantly acting and reacting to what the other agents are doing.

The ideas and models of CAS are grounded in modern biological views on adaptation and evolution. Examples of complex adaptive systems include the stock market, social insect and ant colonies, the biosphere and the ecosystem, the brain and the immune system, the cell and the developing embryo, and any human social group-based endeavor in a cultural and social system such as political parties or communities.

A complex adaptive system behaves/evolves according to three primary principles:

1) **Order is emergent as opposed to predetermined.**

2) **The system's history is irreversible (i.e., you can't change the past, so you learn from it).**

3) **The system's future is often unpredictable.**

There are interesting parallels for more rapid organizational adaptability within the characteristics of complex adaptive systems:

- **Boundaries** are not imposed from outside. The organism is always testing and crossing boundaries, using them as focal points to force needed change for long-term survival. For most organizations, these boundaries represent management hierarchies, department silos, division offices and so forth. Every successful change effort we have seen has established a mandate for cross-functional collaboration through creating common, shared goals.

- **Sub-optimal** means the complex adaptive system does not have to be perfect in order for it to thrive within its environment. It only has to be slightly better than its competitors. Any energy used on being better than that is wasted energy. Once it has reached the state of being good enough, a complex adaptive system will pursue increased efficiency in favor of greater effectiveness. Pareto principle (80-20 rule) anyone? Execution trumps strategy in a fast-moving change environment.

- **Continuous Feedback** is always in place to control the complex adaptive system. Two types of feedback take place – positive and negative – increasing what works, decreasing what doesn't. In business, feedback must link leaders, customers, and employees together.

- **Emergence** (versus planning) is how things get done. Complex adaptive systems follow certain natural laws or rules, but nothing is formally planned in advance. Unpredictability is a natural event in a nonlinear world. When confronted with complex interdependencies, you "emerge" with a solution. (The weather is a complex adaptive system and we adjust our clothing according to local weather forecasts). Emerging in organizations requires close contact with the system we are inter-dependent with – i.e., customers. This does not mean you drop planning, but it means you do it very differently in an environment of rapid change. Shorter, more frequent, more adjustable strategic plans which center around "innovation" are the new standard.

- **Requisite Variety** supports the concept that, the greater the variety within the system, the stronger it is. In a CAS, contradictions create new possibilities to co-evolve with their environment. Democracy is a good example: Its strength is derived from tolerance and even insistence on a variety of political perspectives. Teams with really different members (and methods to tap their points of view) are a powerful way to increase variety, which leads to stronger decisions. (Note: This is not advocating spreading more consensus – we think consensus has become a disease that is slowly weakening our companies. We strongly advocate for ONE decision maker who collects a larger number of points of view, but who holds final authority).

- **Simple Rules** apply since complex adaptive systems are not complicated. The emerging patterns may have a rich variety but, like a kaleidoscope, the rules governing the function of the system are quite simple. A classic example is that all the water systems in the world – all the streams, rivers, lakes, oceans, waterfalls, with their infinite beauty, power and variety – are governed by one simple principle: water finds its own level. One simple operating principle that emerged from a recent client session: *We agree to always look forward.* This one "ground rule" has transformed the way they work.

- **Iteration** means that small changes in the initial conditions of the system can have significant effects after they have passed through the emergence-feedback loop a few times. In his famous research project detailed in *Good to Great*, Jim Collins talked about this as a flywheel: Once you get something in motion, it carries on its own momentum. This in fact, is the very premise of our book.

This book is not a detailed treatise on the subject of complex systems and evolutionary science; but applying these concepts to organizational change will help you move faster:

- Create smaller projects that allow people to sit in a room together and create;

- Schedule shorter meetings that keep energy and ideas fresh;

- Charter teams with fewer members and diverse roles and backgrounds, to ensure many points of view;

- Ensure constant feedback and learning (with direct customer contact) become central elements of the team's work;

- Create a culture in which course-correction and a bias for action are expected; there is no backlash from failure or mistakes. Focus on the future.[29]

Fostering a Culture of Learning

"Learn to fail," said one brilliant mentor, "it will serve you well in your life."

When you approach life as a test, failure is getting the wrong answer – no second chances. Business is fraught with finger pointing, "throwing people under the bus," and public ridicule as a result of a mindset of pass/fail.

When you approach business from a learning mindset, mistakes are a required element toward achievement of mastery (which is never fully realized). You expect to be "not good" for a while. You get better as you practice. Failure is *never* a waste.

Cultivating learning in your team or company is how you ensure lasting growth:

Static Approach	Learning Approach
Life is a test →	Life is a journey of learning →
Pass or fail →	Discovery is the goal →
Avoid risk →	Embrace the new →
Analysis driven →	Feedback driven →
Overlook new growth opportunities →	Experiment, test, shift →
Fail more often in new situations →	Succeed more often in new situations
Reinforcing life is a test	**Reinforcing life is about learning**

Meetings are a territory-rich opportunity for installing a learning mindset.

With a recent client, we embedded a meeting practice in which every session ended with a 5-minute summary: "What did we learn today? How can we improve?" The spirit of the conversation shifts dramatically with this one small change to how they communicate.

What about Mistakes?

Mistakes are at the very base of human thought....feeding the structure like root nodules. If we were not provided with the knack of being wrong, we would never get anything useful done.

— Lewis Thomas. *The Medusa and the Snail*. Viking 1979

What is the purpose of mistakes in learning?

Remember our story from Chapter 5, about victims and offenders facing each other directly to restore the balance in the community? When a government (or a boss or a parent)) overrides the natural system of "cause-effect" that corrects mistakes, you set up a situation in which people seek to cover up the truth. Being afraid to make mistakes – which are an ordinary part of the human experience – perpetuates a culture of fear and hiding.

We believe this is one of the major sources of the rampant trust-depletion that exists between people in our culture.

If your organization is suffering from an environment in which learning is not valued, new ideas are stifled, and risk-taking is taboo, it's almost guaranteed that finger-pointing and lack of trust – however well-disguised they may be – are the underlying cause.

In our story of the technology company, Louis is Bill's right-hand man. He oversees the software development group. He shares his management style to create a focus on learning and action.

Louis' Story

"I am a natural experimenter. When you have a bias for action, you don't have a fear of failure. Failure is doing nothing at all rather than trying something and finding out it didn't work. If someone in my group tries something and fails and they just stop ... *that's* the failure.

You don't know how to do addition when you're born – then you see the symbols and learn the process and you practice. You don't get 100% right out of the gate. Once you've mastered addition, what if you never try anything else? Then you never learn subtraction or multiplication. If someone who works for me tries something and it fails, I expect them to pick themselves up and try again. Because that is the *only* way to learn – you learn from the failures not the successes. When it becomes obvious that something they tried didn't work I say: "Well done, you tried. Now what are you going to do?" I'm expecting to hear: "This is what I'm going to change this time around." The most important thing is to make sure they don't give up. I see my job as helping them to pick themselves up, dust themselves off and try again.

You have to create room for this process. The only way I know how to do that is to fail visibly myself. When I get it wrong, I say (out loud): "I got that wrong." That provides permission for them to do the same. I don't punish anybody for failing. I tell them "Listen, I'm married. I wake up every morning to find out what it was I did wrong yesterday!" You have to learn to accept that you won't get it right from everybody's perspective. Even when I *think* I've gotten it right, I've failed from someone *else's* perspective. In my world, there is no failure and there is no success. There is only getting the job done to the best of your ability, discovering what you learned from it, and moving on.

We're getting down to the wire on a major project – the launch release is 6 weeks out and it's crunch time. When we reach the deadline, we will have done it in one year, which is a massive accomplishment. Roger (the SVP who cares for this product line) is amazed – he is just over the moon happy we made this happen on this timeline. But I expect some of his peers might think it's a failure; that I spent too many resources on this versus something else they cared about more. It doesn't matter how much I get it right, someone else will see what I do as a failure. You have to come to terms with that and do the right thing. And what makes that possible for me to do, is that I know "I got this far, I could start again tomorrow and I'll be OK. I am prepared to go back and sweep floors in the factories if I have to."

And that's what makes me different from those who try to figure it all out in the beginning, in a way that will make everyone happy. I say: "You could have just started rather than spend three months debating it." You cannot treat software development as academic theory. Because the truth is, if you approach each person's needs and disappointments head-on, you learn what they really need.

It's crucial to learn to apologize – quickly. "Maybe I got it wrong – sorry about that. What can I do to help you now?" When you can see people just need to vent about a situation and not AT you, the situation changes immediately. Recently I was talking with someone who claimed a big contract with DOD was on the line if we didn't add a feature. Once I sat down and understood what he was really trying to accomplish, we worked together to define the work and create a schedule, and things turned around.

I have seen a conversation take three hours because people are arguing how we got to where we are, rather than how to move forward from where we are. The moving forward conversation is typically more like 30 minutes. When you shift to the future, the entire conversation changes and usually the problem just melts away. A blame conversation is all about, "You've got the problem," or "I didn't even know that you wanted that." That is the wrong type of conversation. When you move to a forward-looking conversation, things always improve. Learning is all about, "How quickly can we get to that conversation?"

There is someone on my team (Richard) who loves to be right at all costs. Recently we were meeting about the new initiative that is a very important part of our future. Richard focuses on: "I haven't got enough data. I'm not sure where we are... Peter is not doing this, he's not doing that." I get very uncomfortable hearing these kinds of statements – if I'm Peter and I learn Richard is saying these things to my boss, where do we stand on trust?

If you throw your colleague under the bus to save yourself from looking foolish, who ends up looking foolish in the end?"

The path to extinction can be painful and inevitable for some. Take some risks, and find new approaches to organizational evolution. At the very least, you might discover that learning itself is a concept that will never go extinct.

SUMMARY
Nature's Truth #7:

Nature uses learning to avoid extinction.

In business, building a learning culture is the remedy to support an environment of sustainable growth.

There are three principles of embedding an effective learning culture:

(1) Make sure everyone has a shared understanding of the threats and opportunity for the business. The outcome is to create urgency in everyone.

(2) Broaden perspective to detect the need for change, then move faster and adapt more quickly to offset the increasing uncertainty of prediction.

(3) Learn to fail and embed a learning mindset in your organization (see practices below)

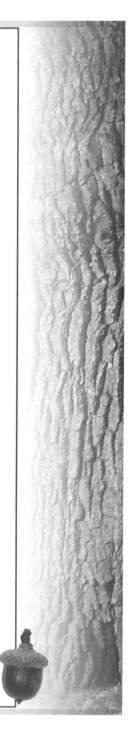

Making It Work! Small Changes for Learning and Avoiding Extinction

Learning mindsets are very powerful. If you translate them into simple behaviors then you can transform a unwieldy, slow-moving elephant into a fast-moving, adaptive gazelle by doing these things:

1. **Get more contact with the outside world: Customers, vendors, competitors. A recent client takes his software programmers on sales calls to customer sites; the customer gets to talk with programmers about what they want and what frustrates them, the programmer gets useful feedback.**

2. **Focus on learning and the future (less about feedback and the past). Remember the meeting practice where every session ends with a 5-minute summary "What did we learn today? How can we improve?"**

3. **Expect your people to stretch *themselves*. Spend time asking your people what *they* are committed to, and reward the people who raise their own expectations. We have a client who does this at the beginning of each year and checks on progress each quarter.**

4. Create learning-focused rules of engagement. Examples of good "learning-focused" operating principles include:

- Everyone has a positive intent (e.g.,, mistakes are not intentional).

- Focus on the future (blame and finger-pointing are past oriented).

- Just do it – test it, adapt it.

- There is no such thing as failure, only feedback.

Create a process by which everyone can interact with a visible, small number of operating principles regularly over time, especially in meetings. Try out the ones listed here, and add your own.

5. Learning means seeking outside points of view.

- Hire a coach

- Build a network of trusted mentors – both inside your company and outside. Have a coffee or lunch date at least once a month with someone outside your organization whom you admire.

- Join a CEO board or master-mind group.

- *Be* a mentor, coach or advisor to someone. Those who teach, learn.

These work best when you have a leader who supports taking risks, facing challenges as opportunities, and testing small changes as the foundation for bigger change.

What did you learn from reading this chapter?

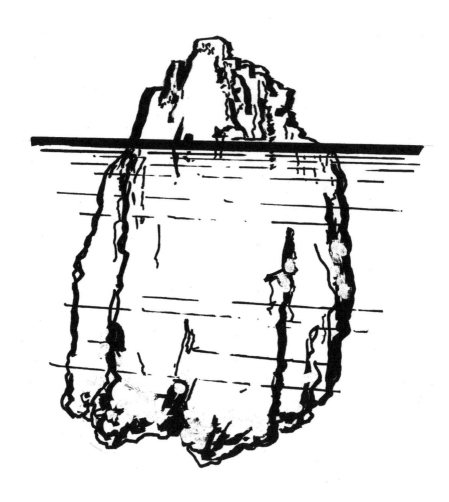

Chapter 8 – MINDSETS
Navigating the Icebergs

Chapter 8 explores the unseen elements that often poison or derail our ability to adapt and change: our mindsets and assumptions, which are largely unconscious, unexplored, and unquestioned. To grow a great culture means a constant willingness to observe and appreciate the diversity within very small assumptions, ways of being creative and managing people. How can you manage territorialism and alpha leadership through changing deeper mindsets that drive those behaviors?

Navigating the Icebergs

Nature's Truth #8:

In nature, the truth may not be obvious
or easy to spot – such as icebergs.

In business, mindsets are the hidden force of
our thinking that keep us stuck or help us change
when progress is needed.

*"The empires of the future are empires
of the mind."*

— Winston Churchill

Most people know Roger Barrister was the first person to run a mile in less than four minutes.

He ran it in 3 minutes, 59.4 seconds on May 6, 1954 on a windy spring day, during an athletic meeting between the British AAA and Oxford University.

Once the four-minute barrier was broken by Roger Bannister, 16 other runners broke the four minute barrier in the 3 years that followed. (Previously the world record had been four minutes, 1.4 seconds, held by Sweden's Gunder Haegg, and had not been beaten for 9 years, since 1945.)

Was Roger an example of a sudden leap in human evolution? What occurred to the *physical* barrier that prevented humans from running the four-minute mile? The breakthrough was not in athleticism, it was the *change in mindset* that made the difference. Bannister showed that breaking the four-minute mile could be done.

Often the reality we believe is really the barriers we perceive. Previous runners subscribed to a prevalent belief that it was impossible to run a mile in under 4 minutes.

Once someone shattered that belief, others could now aspire to reach what was a seemingly impossible goal.[30]

In the business world, daily life is mostly conducted by the credo "I have to see it to believe it."

"Show me the money."

"Prove it to me."

However, in business, it's what you *can't* see that often bites you in the rear. People talk about "culture" as the unchangeable personality of the business that gets in the way of progress. What's at the root of culture? The beliefs and assumptions held by leaders and employees that often reinforce the status quo and allow fear of change to slow progress.

We cheer those hard-earned culture roots! They allow stability, predictability, and a sense of identity. They create tribal belonging for the people who work there.

But left unquestioned in a rapid-changing environment, they sometimes harden into a rigid mass that impedes the organization's ability to adapt. For the leader who is unaware, the comfort zone of "this is how it's always been" can become the iceberg that sinks their unsinkable ship.

What *Are* Mindsets?

Mindsets are like staking out our territory: hard to let go of when they have become familiar. They limit us or expand us. Like the Roger Barrister story, we often are not even aware that we limit possibility by what we believe or don't believe. The most dangerous belief of all? "We're good enough with what we know how to do and the way things are."

This belief is a *significant* factor that holds an organizational culture in place — or allows it to change. It is your "white swan" (see Chapter 7). Having never *seen* a black swan, the assumption is there is only one color of swan (one way to make a profit, one way to launch an initiative, one way to stay competitive).

Understanding how to work with mindsets to build positive expectancy and desire for change has singularly opened the pathway to impossible growth goals in the organizations and individuals we have worked with.

Note: We are not advocating that you start imagining ways to defy the laws of physics. We are saying that often, what you *think* are laws, *aren't*.

In fact, as a result of addressing their mindsets, one of our clients secured a $450 million investment simply by addressing the limiting beliefs they held about their parent company (full story later in the chapter).

All mindsets are not all created equal. The way people hold their belief systems have variable strength depending on the circumstances that created them.

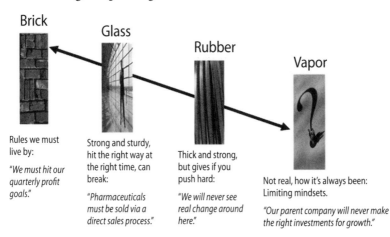

Brick

Rules we must live by:

"We must hit our quarterly profit goals."

Glass

Strong and sturdy, hit the right way at the right time, can break:

"Pharmaceuticals must be sold via a direct sales process."

Rubber

Thick and strong, but gives if you push hard:

"We will never see real change around here."

Vapor

Not real, how it's always been: Limiting mindsets.

"Our parent company will never make the right investments for growth."

Some mindsets are like brick – unmovable. This is the territory of religion and politics. Wars are fought trying to change this level of mindset territory.

Some mindsets are more like glass. They are very strong, but if you tap on them just the right way, they will shatter. The first time my grandmother saw an airplane lift off the ground in the early 1900s, her belief that men cannot fly was immediately shattered.

Some mindsets are like rubber. They may show up as impossible dilemmas – you can have your cake *or* eat it, but not both. One of our clients had a wrenching decision to make about whether to stay in a lucrative corporate job (with two kids to put through college) or pursue her dreams of doing work of the heart. She saw the choices as "either/or." By seeing it that way, she created tremendous conflict internally – a "sucker's choice" (either way I lose something important). It takes skill to find a big enough goal or perspective where all possibilities become real choices, not sucker's choices.

Some mindsets are vapor – invisible and difficult to expose, question or discuss. Like odorless natural gas, they perform their job without you being aware of their existence. Many of our coaching clients come to us with a belief about their limiting behaviors: "This is the way I am." A recent client of Gerry's (let's call him Ashutosh) wanted to be better giving presentations to his board, who were his company's owners. While he was a very competent COO, his board had concerns about how insecure he *seemed* in front of them – even though he had a high degree of technical prowess. "I've always been an introvert, which is why this is so hard for me." This belief prevented him from making changes necessary in previous coaching, a long stint with Toastmasters, and a lot of practice. This limiting belief was indeed toxic vapor! Once we got past it, his progress was rapid and dramatic. After the next board meeting, he said; "Not only do I feel more confident, but my board sees me as more capable. This has changed my career." The CEO was visibly surprised: "Ashutosh has earned our confidence 100% — the shift was remarkable."

When you can shift a group of people toward a **common** mindset about the need for change, in which they all have a vested interest and a belief that change is necessary, meaningful change can happen almost overnight. One of the nonprofits Gerry has worked with began their organization based on a simple and powerful belief that even the most impoverished and underprivileged members of our society will take responsibility for their community's well being and work hard to improve it, given the right support. Their success wasn't overnight, but has exceeded many of their skeptics' expectations.

How Do You Spot a Mindset?

A person's behaviors or words are a marker for a massive iceberg of mindsets, based on past experiences through which they see the world, make decisions, and communicate.

Behaviors and words are the only visible signs for the largely unconscious drivers of our behavior (see diagram: Iceberg). As our iceberg diagram illustrates, some change impacts at the surface and some impacts deeper. Organizations tend to focus on and make changes to the environment (IT systems, processes, organizational structure, etc.) and sometimes behavior (through training, mentoring, or performance management systems). But they rarely see or address what's harder to notice, or below the surface. Still deeper, is the territory of capabilities - what we know *how* to do ("We don't have specific technical skills"); mindsets – our beliefs and assumptions ("We can't learn the skills we need because management won't let us"), and sometimes even our core identity - how we view ourselves or who we think we are ("We really are not a technical team"). What's below the surface is what we are calling markers.

Markers for deeper meaning appear in language such as:

"We can't because…"

"They won't let us…."

"We have to…"

"We must…"

"It would be better if we…"

"I should…."

Whenever you hear what linguists call modal operators, (these examples) you can be sure a belief is not far away.

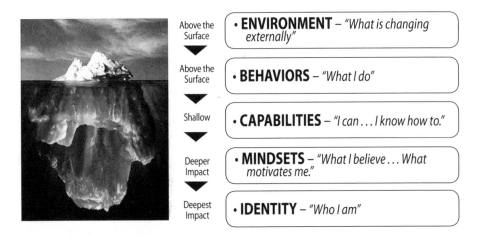

To complicate matters, one person's "marker" for meaning can be completely different from another person's marker. The completely unique combination of our individual experiences, family history and cultural backgrounds means there are approximately 6.5 billion people with their own personalized, subjective icebergs.

As a result, creating "shared meaning and action" in today's diverse, fast-changing workplaces is like navigating a ship through an iceberg field without GPS – fraught with unseen, unknown elements. When moving at high speeds - as the Titanic proved - this can lead to disaster. Captain Smith was one of the most highly trained senior captains in the White Star Line. Based on his experience and reputation, it became routine for Smith to command the Line's newest ships on their maiden voyage. He was chosen to lead Titanic on its first voyage as an honor – it was to be his final voyage before retirement. Given that, the important question is "Why did Captain Smith appear to ignore signals he surely received about the dangers lurking in the cold seas – and instead keep his ship moving at high speed through a known ice field?" There will never be a certain answer to this question - but the question itself is a powerful one that any wise leader will ask regularly inside their team or organization. "What signals of danger are we missing or ignoring?" "What black swans are we assuming can only be white?"

Change is a process of learning, as we discussed in Chapter 7. Conditions change in nature, and plants or animals either adapt or don't. In an organization, adapting is a conscious process of questioning beliefs, assumptions, and mindsets. It requires fostering a conscious discipline to ensure you are seeking and listening to the right knowledge, so you can adapt quickly in unseen, unknown territory. In a global economy, fostering collaborative, cross-functional and cross-geographical dialogue is how you gain a broad enough perspective to do that. Keep your eyes and ears open, ask enough questions, and someone almost always has the right answer: "The sea is flat calm tonight. We need to slow down so we can spot the icebergs in time to avoid them." Too many leaders guide their "ships" onto illogical paths that leave people scratching their heads, or worse, take their team or company down by innocently (or not) ignoring wisdom that sits within earshot. Jim Collins refers to this as "hubris." In this chapter, we take a deeper look at what lies beneath the tendency to hold onto beliefs and mindsets that are no longer useful, sufficient or relevant.

Let's illustrate this phenomenon through an example. Suppose a colleague, Christina, says to you (her boss): "I want to feel secure in my job." For Christina, this statement is a "marker" for the following belief: "I want to have the freedom to explore new ideas and learn new skills without fear of interference from a micromanaging boss."

For you, these words are a marker for "I want guaranteed employment."

Because we are mostly not *consciously aware* of our markers (the meaning behind our thoughts), without really thinking, we map our markers onto other people. It's sort of like your brain is an LCD projecting your pictures onto someone else's wall. In Christina's statement, you probably *assume or believe* Christina's comment means she wants guaranteed employment, without even being aware of that assumption. You create meaning in her comment based on *your* marker, not hers.

If you don't take the time to ask "Christina, what does secure mean to you?" your behavior toward Christina plays out based on your marker – which has nothing to do with what Christina meant. This probably results in a gulf of misunderstanding between you and Christina.

This disconnect may seem obvious for anyone trained in basic communication, but the tricky element is the lack of awareness most of us have about our thoughts and expectations, and how we unconsciously project them onto others. We communicate the majority of the time without ever clarifying what another person's markers really mean. We assume Christina wants guaranteed employment, and our behavior follows. As Christina's boss, your actions toward her may be colored by that assumption. Christina's real intention – the desire for increasing freedom to explore – is never discussed.

Now, imagine that you say: "We are acquiring X company as an opportunity to grow into the solutions and service space, and we must strategically evolve our technologies to capitalize on this." How many meanings could you extract from this statement? (This is an actual vision from one client; we couldn't find a single leader inside the organization who could simply explain what it really meant, and nobody at the employee level had any knowledge of what leaders wanted them to *do* about it.) Leaders and employees in this organization sincerely want their company to succeed, but when they don't take time to create shared meaning so people's mindsets "match up," it's unlikely that aligned action will happen quickly enough.

Our workplaces today are a melting pot of misunderstood intentions and mindsets about people's motives, intentions, and meaning.

In our expert opinion, THIS is one of the most common root causes behind failed change. Lack of clarity and shared meaning is a crimp in the hose of innovative ideas in almost every company, despite the plethora of consulting firms, books, and trainings attempting to provide road maps to manage change. Legacy mindsets, limiting beliefs, and black swan assumptions are the reason a team or organization reverts to old behaviors and habits even after a change has been in motion for some period of time.

Aligning large numbers of people toward a common and clearly understood goal is a highly skilled process. It starts by knowing there is deeper meaning behind everything we say and do. It is a learned skill to reveal and discuss the meaning beneath our markers to avoid misinterpretation and guesswork. It is an act based on the intention for *real* understanding. And, it requires skill to do it in a way that doesn't threaten people or become a psychological distraction to the important work of the organization.

On the other hand, often a simple change to the environment is enough to shift behavior and easily transform what seems a complex problem into a simple solution. In their book *Influencer: The Power To Change Anything,*[31] the authors relate a case study about Emory Air Freight, in which only 45% of the air freight containers were being completely filled. Consultants puzzled over the best change management process to drive people's behavior to fill the containers. The ultimate solution? The president drew a red line and wrote "Fill to Line" on the outside of the containers. Within 24 hours, more than 90% of the containers were being filled.

The point? A tremendously powerful small change everyone can make, is to examine your assumptions and stories and be open to adapting them. The simplest way? Experiment! Set up simple ways to test new ideas – and also to learn whether your existing assumptions are *really* true.

Can You Change a Mindset?

As we explored in Chapter 5, people aren't machines you can retool by switching out parts. Belief systems don't change easily, especially when one cannot see a personal benefit (corporate revenue and profit rarely are enough). To treat people's deeply held beliefs as such would be manipulative and borders on unethical.

At the same time, we have seen leaders successfully build a change-friendly culture by skillfully reframing the meaning of people's roles and contributions to be opportunistic, positive, and empowered. This is *all* about impacting mindsets, and shaping them to be more positive.

And, it requires practice, patience, and persistence.

Remember our iceberg model?

You have to be aware of how the environment – and people's behavior – reinforces the existing mindsets or culture. Change efforts tend to focus on:

1. **Who will have what jobs?**

2. **What positions will be posted?**

3. **What buildings will be closed?**

4. **Who will the window offices be given to?**

5. **How will my daily routine change?**

But during a merger or other big change initiative it's essential to question our identity and outdated practices. In fact, most change initiatives require counterintuitive moves. And if you don't question the existing ways of working, you will end up with a powerful force of inertia to overcome (remember Newton's Laws from Chapter 6). Leaders have to make space for that opportunity to discuss: "Who do we want to become?" "How do we want to move forward, to bring out the best in both entities?" "What works for us, and what doesn't?"

By discussing the questions and issues people hold during change, you send a signal that how we work together is as important as making money.

This happens only by setting up a process for it – remember that mindsets are not visible or thought about on a day-to-day basis by people. In working with one of our clients, we designed a series of employee meetings in which people presented their ideas about the ideal organizational structure. Leaders met 1:1 with a handful of people in the organization to find out what they really feel their contribution could be. Everyone was given "immunity" to say whether they preferred to opt out within the next 6-12 months – which meant they would not be fired immediately, but they would be on the list to receive a fair package. (Many people will do so when they feel it's safe.) Simple benchmark surveys are next, along with focus groups. For a few months, you start meetings with a reference to the "new vision," – a simple one or two sentences that connect the meeting to the larger vision. (remember Bill's story from Chapter 2).

Change *expresses* itself in the behavior and the environment (through actions leaders take). But what *produces* successful change occurs within the mindsets people hold about the situation or change. It's less about the reality and more about the story we tell ourselves about what it means.

Melissa was a coaching client. She held a belief she could not be "trusted" to be a real leader. She held the passion, the vision, the people skills; but she felt she didn't have what it took to "jump in with both feet" and make it happen. When we explored the root of that belief, we discovered a memory of an experience from years prior. One day, she was in a swimming pool with her 2-year-old daughter, who began to wade in too deep. Instead of jumping toward her, she held back and waited for her husband to react. In her mind, that tiny incident had become a symbol of a tendency to wait before acting, even when a situation was urgent. How could such a person be a good leader? Through a simple process of reframing this belief, she was able to see that hesitancy is contextual – "think first, then act" has a place in leadership. Even if it were a weakness (hesitancy) it did not define her as a leader. By naming it and considering where it was useful, it allowed hesitancy to become a *tool* in her kit, versus a limitation. This process is not always about revisiting your childhood; in a team, it can be as simple as asking a few questions to heighten awareness about the belief, and facilitating a process that helps people consciously discuss what mindset or beliefs would be more useful to reaching the team's goals.

Especially when a change has a negative impact (e.g., layoffs, pay cuts or plant closures), we urge leaders to put more attention on helping people discuss and shift negative mindsets *about* what the situation means. Otherwise, you may see short-term compliance based on people's desire to obey, but fear has a way of accumulating mass below the surface. What sustains transformation over time is a conscious, collective story of the necessity and positive benefits of change – this is necessary to overcome the limiting beliefs people hold within themselves.

Exposing mindsets and discussing them openly is like turning on a flashlight in a dark cave. The illumination helps people see, and accept, what's really going on. It may not change what's in the cave, but at least you know what you're dealing with. This is a very important concept in shifting to a positive mindset about change.

In the earlier chapters, we talked about the importance of vision, trust, planning, decision rights, collaboration, and communication. But no methods, processes or systems will have "sticking power" if you don't surface and address mindsets that hold the team or organization in the past.

A change-friendly leader will gently and firmly guide people and teams to get to know and trust each other, and discover their own "markers" for meaning to create a positive orientation toward change.

A powerful example of this occurred in one of our clients – an executive team of a successful company with a 70-year track record of growing revenue and profit – and "owning" the majority of market share in their industry. Part of their success was the result of being in a tightly regulated industry, which meant there was almost no competition in the U.S. market. As is often the case, this lack of competition had made them internally focused, not customer centric, and slow to innovate. In 2000, they were acquired by a large company in their industry. After the acquisition, the parent company noticed some of these "insular" traits and began imposing infrastructure requirements in a misguided attempt to reign in what they saw as a "cowboy culture." The result? A significant erosion of profit margins and a lot of whining from the acquired company's executive team. Their meetings sometimes derailed into gripe sessions about how bad the parent company was: "They limit our future;" "We'll never succeed if they don't leave us alone;" and so on.

After months of trying to expose the team's underlying mindsets about the relationship with the parent, Lisa cracked it open over breakfast with the President. While neither of us can remember the exact question she asked, we both will never forget the huge "AHA" that resulted. The President realized in that moment, the impact of his and his team's beliefs. And that was where real transformation began. Once he saw it, he was relentless in helping his team achieve a similar understanding. In the year following that breakfast meeting, the relationship with the parent truly did transform, resulting in a $450M investment to support their aggressive growth mission.

What changed was not a result of conflict management or negotiation training, nor was it somehow that the parent company finally beat them into submission.

The combination of right timing, enough pain and urgency, and the ability of an outside perspective changed one person's willingness to make the most important change: within himself.

Once that happens, the path forward usually unfolds with more ease and grace.

To illustrate, let's revisit Dan's challenge to change the mindsets in his own company, plagued with a lot of doubts and fears around, "This can't be done." While people believed that it was possible to build software within the cost and time constraints it took to be competitive, most people did not believe it was possible inside this organization. There was simply too much evidence from the past, of having tried and failed. One of the most important mindset shifts Dan faced was building trust in the people and the process, before the evidence showed it could be done (the "proof" was going to take several years!)

Dan had to answer the question that was prevalent in people's minds, but remained largely unasked: "What makes it different this time?" That took his being willing to speak openly about the small changes they had made:

- **First, placing new leaders in charge of the software development group who had a track record of building software within cost and time guidelines.**

- **Second, finding an example within their company of having made that exact journey for another part of the business.**

- **Third, chartering a cross-functional team with high visibility and accountability to clear goals and short-term milestones. No more than 6 months would go by without sharing results in Town Hall forums that anyone in the company could attend.**

- Lastly (and perhaps most importantly), the evidence that they had dedicated resources to this initiative by removing people from existing projects to focus on this one.

None of these "points of evidence" by itself would have sufficiently reframed the mindset; but by Dan continuing to patiently remind people of these steps, he was able to turn the tide so that the dominant mindset is now: "I see that it's possible. How can we make this work?"

Change-Derailing Mindsets

As we learned in Chapter 6 on Communication, the change landscape in organizations today is fraught with confusion, and the "pull to the left" (cynicism) is usually stronger than the "pull to the right" (commitment). In any team or organization, people are quick to jump to the worst case scenario; to assign bad intentions to their leaders; to cry "ain't it awful" more than they do "what's possible for us to accomplish together?"

There are several common mindsets that are poisonous to change:

1) **We know best.** Our executives are paid large salaries and bonuses to have the answers, not ask questions. This is the poison that leads to hubris. Organizations with this mindset create cultures that don't value candor and open dialogue – and as a result, they ignore signals from the market that change is needed, usually until it is too late. Think Enron. The antidote? A leader who seeks to learn will ask questions, take people's input to heart, and focus everything around the customer. One of the more brilliant public examples of this? Lou Gerstner's turnaround at IBM.

2) **We have to do it all.** This is the classic "do more with less" dilemma. It currently exists in many large organizations in decline, characterized by a culture of over-committed people and burnout. There is no focused strategy - nor is there relentless prioritization against a clear strategy. Organizations ingesting this poison chase the flavor-of-the-month and new opportunities without regard to whether they can execute well. As a result, they usually don't. The antidote? Go on a project diet: put several projects or initiatives that aren't connected to the top three objectives and strategies on the back burner.

3) **Life is a test.** "A" grades are the measure of learning. If you flunk, you've failed. When leaders fail at an initiative, they are punished. This is the opposite of the "growth mindset" – which is about growing intellectual and knowledge capital, not just sales and market share. Related to #1, this mindset creates a culture of "right answers" and fear. It is common in academic or research-based companies. Innovation and risk-taking are given lip service but not embedded into the culture beyond R&D, nor is there a process or system that ensures innovation is a widespread mindset across the team or organization. The antidote? Read Chapter 7 and make some small changes to adopt learning mindsets and practices in your team or department.

4) **Profit cannot be compromised.** This is a classic leadership either/or mindset: e.g., "Either we meet our numbers or we invest in developing our people." "If we don't hold our people accountable we'll never meet our numbers." This poison usually does not manifest by a small dose of occasional belt-tightening, but is a culture that lives and dies by the numbers, is plagued by short-term thinking, and "blank stares" come back when you ask leaders about long-term vision. This type of company often sees increasing turnover as talented people go where they can make a more meaningful contribution, weary of the ruthless focus on squeezing more from a dry lemon. The antidote? If you are leading in this culture and want to change, start investing in your people's development. Chances are they are incredibly thirsty for it.

5) **We've always done it this way.** Rarely stated, this poison pill takes the form of elaborate and well-justified resistance to new ideas, nostalgic references to "when can we get back to the way it used to be," and lack of willingness to adopt new processes and procedures. This culture is common in large, legacy organizations or entitled environments that have never had to change. The antidote? Urgency – usually around survival – is the only way you get people moving in this culture, and it requires a strong, visionary, committed leader.

6) **We can do it ourselves.** The poison in this mindset is "asking for help" – a tremendous sign of weakness. Reaching across boundaries (within our company, with vendors, with customers, with consultants) weakens power because we tip our hand or give up knowledge. The culture traps are similar to #1 and #2; this style is very common in entrepreneurial organizations. The antidote? Infuse new leadership on the team, or charter a small collaborative team project with a defined goal that shows everyone that people can achieve more if they work together.

7) **Because I said so.** "I have the authority and if I say it, nobody had better question it." This poison creates a culture of fear and non-responsibility. Employees treat leaders as parental authority and often seek to undermine in sneaky ways, while leaders wield authority like a big stick, commanding obedience. The antidote? New leadership who carry a more egalitarian and grown-up view of how a workplace should work.

One of the most powerful roles a change agent can play is to help an organization surface and examine unquestioned mindsets that poison change and assist people in moving past them. This can be a difficult process and requires a strong leader with the courage to be transparent and vulnerable (which is driven by their beliefs that learning is the most important mindset to embed into the culture). The team or organization usually will not open up to these conversations unless the leader does it first.

Change-Friendly Mindsets

At their core nature, human beings are a curious species. Learning has a universal pull for every person regardless of title, position, or vocation.

Change-friendly mindsets are a GPS system for navigating through transitions gracefully. There are six mindsets we seek to embed into daily work habits that support more rapid adaptability to change:

1. **Learning is the game.** As discussed in Chapter 7, learning is how nature avoids extinction. In an organization, a leader who is a teacher cultivates wisdom, teaches trust, and understands the need for detachment. This is about being open to all options, which requires being comfortable with uncertainty – and knowing there are "black swans" on the horizon: undiscovered treasures, or serious threats. Life will always deliver the unexpected - so trying to control the uncontrollable is a losing game. If you have difficulty with surprises or are overly stuck on fixed perspectives or control, you will not create an environment in which learning is important and discoveries can unfold. Environments such as this tend to be "stuck in place" rather than adaptive and open to change. One powerful action a leader can take to help people get unstuck and move toward a learning environment is to ask the question: "What is our purpose … and what is one small change we CAN DO – or stop doing - right now, to move us toward it?"

2. Every behavior has a **positive intent**. When someone makes a decision that is less than ideal or thoughtless, we often go straight to judgment. This erodes trust. When you automatically separate behavior from intention – and BELIEVE it - the "on guard" undertow in relationships, especially with difficult people, melts away. It gets replaced by an attitude of problem-solving, curiosity, perhaps even service. Instead of figuring out how to manipulate or control someone into behaving or following the rules, you wonder instead: "What does that person *really* want, and how can I help them get it?" What would

happen in today's businesses and families if everyone moved through their day with "What does that person really want and how can I help them get it?" as the central question in their mind? The CIO of one of the World's largest technology companies changed the culture of his department through the principle of positive intent - by repeatedly asking the question when there was a mistake: "So-and-so did not wake up this morning to be stupid or thoughtless. I wonder what their real intention was?" This one simple but powerful change was soon adopted as a common practice, and it shifted the culture of his organization.

3. **Everything has a season.** Notice the timing of life: There is a beginning, middle and end. Winter doesn't mean death; it is a time to rest and re-group for growth. A leader's job during winter (a decline in revenue or growth) is to help the team reevaluate and ready themselves for the next stage. Spring is a good time for pruning deadwood and rebirth. A leader's job is to help people be creative and focus on unseen or potential opportunity. Summer is about growth. A leader's job is to keep people on track and inspired. Fall is the process of shedding. A leader's job is to courageously help people let go of the past and evaluate what's not needed anymore. Speaking of Fall, the concept of a "Project Diet" – a pruning of the projects and initiatives that no longer serve the current crucial strategies – is a very important practice that we use with almost every client.

4. **There is more opportunity in possibility.** Think *realistic possibility.* You will have a greater ability to improve your environment from "what's possible" than from "what's wrong" and "what doesn't work." It's not about being unwilling to accept reality in the present. It is about being willing to see what you can do to make the situation better – there's *always* something. When people are whining, practice asking simple, positive, future-focused questions: "How can we?"" "What if?" "What is one small change we can make, that's within our control?" and watch what happens.

5. **United we stand, divided we fall.** When you catalyze alignment, excitement, and energy among a *group* of people across an organization, your goals will move faster. The more diverse the interests and backgrounds, the more work it takes, but the bigger the payoff in terms of support, innovation, and cooperation. The Starbucks story from Chapter 2 is a great example – that one little store didn't need corporate sanction; they just created a stretch goal and got everyone excited on the team to make it happen. They used team pride as the catalyst for change.

6. **Expect obstacles.** If you are navigating through heavy iceberg territory, expect obstacles. The leader's job is to help people stay calm and focused to solve problems effectively, not ignore them, bully through them, or allow the drama of tension and conflict to prevail. It's about believing that obstacles exist and they are part of the journey. The next time you are tired, beaten down, and ready to quit – call your "intention cheerleader" or anyone who can help you remember obstacles are part of any worthy endeavor.

These six mindsets require the willingness and ability to reframe our existing situation.

Mindset Change in Action

A senior executive Gerry worked with oversaw a budget of about $1 billion. He had important insights and expertise on how to architect a strategic win in the business. Unfortunately, nobody else at his level, or above, could really hear them. He was viewed as "cold" and "self-serving." He had a habit of talking over people. Gerry had just spent about 6 hours establishing the coaching relationship and trying to understand this executive's mindset. It turned out to be typical of many corporate leaders: "In my world, you get further by being right than by being liked. Being right is the pathway by which you ascend in the corporate world."

Our intent has a funny way of perpetuating behaviors that got attention in childhood. This executive wanted to be successful and wanted his company to be successful. He had studied leadership from all the great sources, had received the same feedback on many 360's, and even used a corporate coach, as well as a therapist. His *intention* was strong but his *attention* was imbalanced – like yin and yang, he focused too much on one side of the equation.

As a result, instead of being the heir apparent in a multi-billion dollar enterprise, he was at risk of being cast aside in the corporate version of Siberia. His ideas were crucial to the future strategy of the business, but because nobody could get past his arrogance and renegade behavior, they might never be used. People appreciated his brilliant insights, but avoided him because of his seeming self-importance.

After a change in his mindsets (moving toward a few that are change friendly), he called Gerry to report that something odd was happening: People were actually stopping in the hall and talking with him. His relationship with his wife and children was improving. When his boss was re-interviewed a couple of months later, he remarked on what appeared to be a personality transplant. "He seems to have softened, is more available, and people are definitely trusting him more. It's hard to believe how much he's changed and how fast."

Recent contact with him tells us the change continues to this day.

We feel privileged to witness such significant transformations based on our coaching process around changing mindsets. However, the successes are more about the readiness of the leader than about our process. We have had experiences where we have brought all the skills, tools, and processes we know to do, but the person was not ready for a meaningful change. If you are not open enough to see where you are in your own way, you are not willing to discover a better way. If you see change or feedback as a threat, you retract and protect. When that happens, nature will take its course – and you may just find yourself in a fight for survival.

SUMMARY
Nature's Truth #8:

In nature, the truth may not be obvious or easy to spot – such as icebergs.

In business, mindsets are the hidden force of our thinking that keep us stuck or help us change when progress is needed.

- During change, organizations tend to focus on observable elements: the environment and behavior. Beneath these observable elements are hidden mindsets — the capabilities, mindsets, and identities held by leaders and employees that either reinforce the status quo and allow fear of change to slow progress, or accelerate progress to the desired future.

- Mindsets have varying strengths – are yours brick, glass, rubber or vapor? Some are harder to change than others.

- Like "Black Swans," we must remain open to the possibility that something might even exist that could transform everything.

- There are change-derailing and change-friendly mindsets: Learn to notice which are around you and which are in you!

Making It Work! Small Changes for Building Change-Friendly Mindsets

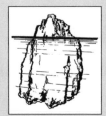

1. Notice where people may have limiting mindsets; you can hear it and see it. Listen and look for:

   "We can't because…"

   "They won't let us…"

   "We have to…"

   "We must…"

   "It would be better if we…"

   "I should…"

2. When you hear change-derailing mindsets, consider what other mindsets you might use that are more useful and empowering, such as:

   "What would happen if we did…?"

   "What if they would let us…?"

   "What would happen if we tried…?"

   "What if we didn't…?"

   "What other options haven't we considered?"

   "What do you think their intention really is?"

"What are you trying to accomplish by doing this?"

"Are you getting the result you wanted?"

3. Quite possibly the most important mindset to explore is your own – about noticing and working with mindsets. Getting started is not as hard as you might think. A participant in a recent "Leading Change" workshop sent us an email describing his use of some of the tools he had learned.

Don's Story

"The other day I was facilitating a group with scattered thoughts trying to solve a problem, which really was more about venting on how bad the situation was and how the industry was forcing them into a space where we had no experience.

"I began a series of probing questions like, 'What is it you're trying to accomplish?' 'What is it you need/want?' 'After you've worked through this, what will that get you? Is that what you wanted?'

"We were able to help boil down a few next steps for clear progress and send a proposal up the management chain.

I still get excited when I see your tools work so nicely."

In our opinion, this situation worked not because of the magic of the questions, but because of the timing – of allowing the "venting" to occur, then someone noticing it and firmly steering the conversation to a useful outcome.

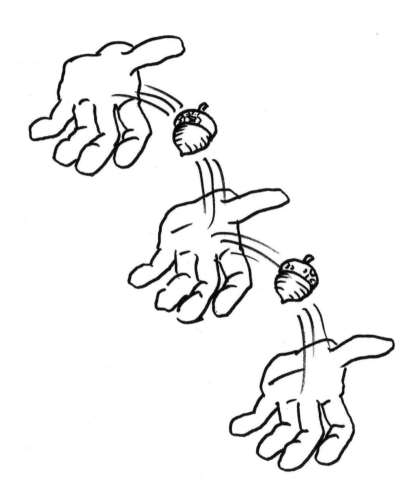

Chapter 9: PROCREATE
Spread Leadership DNA.

Chapter 9 explores the role of leaders in spreading their DNA so that there are more people leading, more often, toward a common purpose and goals. How do you repeat and model the behavior you *want*, over and over?

Spread Leadership DNA

Nature's Truth #9:

In nature, survival is about passing on your DNA.

In business, leaders are the carriers of DNA
and need to see a fundamental part of their job
as passing it on to the next generation.

*"What you leave behind is not what is engraved in
stone monuments, but what is woven into the lives
of others."*

— **Pericles**

"It needs to be unloaded by the end of the day!" (a clear goal if there ever was
one).

We all looked at each other, five young transport company yard hands assigned
to unload a gargantuan boxcar filled with 40-pound sacks of flour. I overheard one
of my co-workers mumble, "He must be joking!"

It was one of those dog days of summer, with the temperature and humid-
ity both in the 90s. We all knew that inside the 50-foot long metal boxcar the

temperature would be well over 100 miserable, sweaty degrees. No one even dared to venture a guess on how many sacks of flour the boxcar contained.

"All right, gentlemen, we're going to do this is in bucket-brigade fashion," said Mac, our new gang boss, a stocky, ruddy-faced, barrel-chested Scot who none of us knew very well.

He stood beside us

As we grumbled and slowly lined up to form our bucket brigade, Mac did an astonishing thing. Instead of assigning himself to some sanitized, rah-rah leadership role, he took off his shirt, climbed into the super-heated boxcar and started passing sacks of flour to the next man in line.

There was no "bully management" going on here. In fact, Mac never belittled any of us for our initial grumbling. He recognized that what we were all about to do was going to be hard work.

And no coaxing or cajoling was necessary. We all knew what we had to do. Mac simply set an expectation by clearly defining our goal right from the start and worked alongside us the entire time, until we got the job done.

He took care of us

Over the next several hours Mac rotated us so that no one was in the boxcar for more than 15 or 20 minutes. He also made sure we took several breaks and drank plenty of water so we wouldn't get dehydrated, which sent the message that he was looking out for us.

He made it fun

Mac's energy, quick wit and humor made us all laugh and joke. After a while, we even broke into song—despite the fact that flour seeping from some of the burlap sacks and mixing with the perspiration on our shirtless bodies was turning us into white, ghoulish-looking creatures. But we simply considered it part of the job. In fact, our pasty appearance served to bond us together, identified us as a unit—especially during breaks, when we mingled with those who were not assigned to our gang.

He made us a team

Intentionally or not, Mac had effectively transported us psychologically from what we considered our daily routine task of mindless lifting and toting to something that resembled a meaningful endeavor.

Soon we were no longer passing sacks of flour to each other—but tossing them. We were no longer a pack of disgruntled yard hands eagerly awaiting the workday's end, but rather a team working together on a mission toward a common goal.

He appreciated us

We unloaded that boxcar in record time. After we had accomplished our goal, Mac thanked us and bought us soft drinks to slake our thirst as we laughingly shared stories of the day.

I doubt any of our fellow yard hands worked as hard as we did that day, certainly none looked as ghastly—and I dare say, none felt as engaged or had the same sense of ownership in their work.

I went to sleep that night with a profound sense of satisfaction and accomplishment—and with a lesson in leadership that I remember to this day, more than 30 years later.

Mac successfully mapped out a hero's journey for a bunch of unmotivated, minimum-wage, twenty something-year-old yard hands tasked with unloading sacks of flour on a scorching hot summer's day —and we responded. As leaders, just imagine what you could do!

A Hero's Journey

This tale of a real-life personal story of a friend Larry Checco, whom we met during the research of this book is both humble and inspiring, showing us how ordinary events can become extraordinary in the presence of a true leader.

He was inspired by the book *The Hero with a Thousand Faces* by renowned mythology scholar, Joseph Campbell, who describes "the hero's journey" whereby ordinary people endure extraordinary hardships, become transformed in the process and achieve the status of hero.

According to Campbell, this story is so fundamental to human existence that it pre-dates Greek mythology, and to this day continues to be told again and again. (Think *Rocky*, *Star Wars*, *Wizard of Oz*, *Harry Potter* — fictional heroes who have made their way into our cultural subconscious). We all love heroes. We all secretly want to be the person with superpowers that can change our own lives or the lives of others. And we know that behind every great hero are those who inspired, supported, and enabled the hero to play her role.

Today, we have elevated leaders into imaginary heroes based on their star quality. Leaders are too often made heroes because they are celebrities, not for the grandeur of their ideas or impact on the world. We believe there is a direct link between this "false hero" phenomenon and the high failure rates of change. Leaders who are placed on a pedestal and rewarded for short-term monetary measures of success have a harder time carrying out a long-term vision and developing a culture that gives others more credit than they take. And yet, these are exactly the qualities of leadership needed to become a change-resilient, adaptive company.

We are in desperate need of a new kind of heroic leadership – which is less about the *hero* and more about the many heroic deeds. Leaders who are courageous and committed to a vision AND to expanding acts of leadership around them, inspire other people to do the same for the people around them. We need leaders who see their role as inspiring heroic actions and decisions every day in others. This is how lasting change will take hold. The ability to adapt on an ongoing basis will depend on leaders who cultivate this across the business.[32]

DNA: How nature conveys competitive advantage

In the natural world, passing on survival characteristics through DNA is how a species adapts and sustains itself long term.

It's no different in the business world. An organization's success in adapting to a faster-moving world requires more leaders who consciously take time to pass on the building blocks of their success to grow more leaders. You can describe the most important job of an adaptive or collaborative leader very simply: Develop yourself so you can develop others.

In *Leaders at All Levels,* Ram Charan contends "Crisis may be an overused word, but it's a fair description of the state of leadership in today's corporations. CEOs are failing sooner and falling harder, leaving their companies in turmoil. At all levels, companies are short on the quantity and quality of leaders they need."

In talking about what's needed, Charan refers to the "first law of holes." When you're in one, stop digging. He says that traditional leadership practices are not working, and we must reinvent our approaches. He thinks about leadership as an apprenticeship model: You identify people who should be developed to achieve leadership mastery and provide them with a clear pathway (including experiences and skills) to ensure their potential *becomes* mastery.

Mr. Charan, we could not agree more. (See box)

Traditional methods for "better-cheaper-faster" are relatively known and easy to copy. The only thing your competitors can't easily replicate is your culture, which is about procreating the spread of great leadership. If you over-spend your time "doing the work" at the expense of "developing people," one day you will be in the unfortunate predicament of the pig who built his house from straw. It was faster, easier and cheaper up front, but unlikely to withstand the huffs and puffs of the big bad competitors.

What the Best Companies Do

In an era of economic uncertainty, the best companies don't give up on developing their leaders; they change how they identify leaders and grow them. They get even more focused and targeted – fewer broad-brush classroom learning programs, more focused methods of developing people on the job, more mentoring and coaching. Learning is directly tied to organizational goals, cost pressures, customer expectations, and limited resources.

In 2009, for the 4th time in 8 years, Fortune magazine teamed with Hewitt Associates and RBL Group to conduct a comprehensive study of the "Top Companies for Leaders." To create the ranking, 500 global companies were surveyed in search of the top businesses at attracting, retaining, and nurturing talent. A team of respected judges from around the world was chosen to help select the final list. The companies that made the cut have one thing in common: They know that investing in their employees isn't a luxury — it's a necessity.

Highlights of best practices from the report:

WALK, NOT JUST TALK

IBM – the #1 company in the Fortune "Top Companies for Leaders 2009" report, invested $700 million last year in leadership development. About 60,000 employees (out of nearly 400,000) are either in leadership position or have the potential to be — representing an investment of almost $12,000 per person.

That is .6% of IBM's total 2009 revenues.

The average company might offer several hundred employees an international opportunity for 2 or 3 years; IBM gives "mobility assignments" to thousands for three to six months.

"It's an investment," says Ted Hoff, vice president with the company's Center for Learning and Development. "We want all IBM leaders to have cross-geographic experience."

Titan Cement (Construction, Greece). Employees early in their careers go through what the company calls the "Career Pre-heater," a one-year program that features 432 hours of training on technological and leadership skills, as well as counseling on how professionals should behave.

"We have a very strongly articulated value system," says CEO Dimitri Papalexopoulos, "which we use as a basis for evaluating not only people but also the way we do business in our day to day operation."

Hindustan Unilever (Mumbai) - This consumer goods company likes to think of itself as a talent factory. And with more than 1,000 alumni sitting on boards globally, it can certainly make a strong case for that.

The company uses what it calls a "70-20-10" model for developing its workforce: 70% of learning happens on the job, 20% through mentoring, and 10% through training and coursework.

That's why employees go through a job rotation roughly every three years, bosses are measured on how well they coach their direct reports, and all employees take about a week's worth of leadership training and four e-learning courses every year.

The company says that senior management spends 30% to 40% of its time grooming leaders.

GROW FROM WITHIN

Proctor & Gamble may be known for its stellar management, but it's the new talent that the company really cultivates.

The company hires less than 1% of the more than half million applicants it screens every year. Excluding entry-level positions, less than 5% of P&G's workforce comprises external hires

ICICI (Banking, Mumbai) doesn't just have recruiters trolling for talent outside of the company; it also has 600 employees who act as talent scouts internally, identifying coworkers with leadership potential.

These internal recruiters tap 5,000 candidates a year, and a panel reviews a profile of each prospective leader and assigns a grade.

SERVE

Leadership training goes beyond the walls of the **General Mills** headquarters. The company has built community service into its culture, with 82% of employees doing some sort of volunteer work.

"Your first year on the job you may not get a billion-dollar brand to run," says Chief Learning Officer Kevin Wilde, "but you could have a significant leadership role in the United Way."

MENTOR

McKinsey is obsessive about growing leaders, not just cultivating talent for the company but also for the public, social, and private sectors beyond McKinsey.

So far, it's got an impressive track record, with many of its 20,000 alumni graduating to leadership positions globally, among them Facebook COO Sheryl Sandberg, newly named Morgan Stanley CEO James Gorman, and Susan Rice, the U.S. Ambassador to the United Nations.

McKinsey places a big emphasis on mentorship, so much so that partners receive feedback on how many consultants refer to them as "mentors." And Managing Director Dominic Barton leads by example: According to the company, he spends 60% of his time mentoring and developing his staff.

EVOLVE

GE is the #1 company in the world in developing leaders. As an example of apprenticeship as the foundation of leadership development, here is their leadership criteria:

1. Create an external focus that defines success in market terms.

2. Be clear thinkers who can simplify strategy into specific actions, make decisions, and communicate priorities.

3. Have imagination and courage to take risks on people and ideas.

4. Energize teams through inclusiveness and connection with people, building both loyalty and commitment.

5. Develop expertise in a function or domain, using depth as a source of confidence to drive change.

In the interest of changing with the times, six months ago, the company [GE] started to examine what it means to be a leader in the 21st century.

GE instituted "leadership dialogues" to look at the issue, and participants ranged from top management to academics. Conversations have focused on the importance of networking, defining company stakeholders more broadly, and inspirational leadership.

And though the results aren't finalized just yet, the company plans to incorporate the findings into its leadership development process.[33]

Leadership and DNA

Remember the concept of "horizontal transfer" from Chapter 7 — the phenomenon in nature by which genes are passed back and forth directly (primarily in bacteria) which allows faster evolution? From this, we can draw an interesting parallel for an apprentice model of leadership as a foundation for organizational change.

Culture is the DNA of an organization – the blueprint that ensures its uniqueness is passed on (even when "sub-cultures" exist, you have a unique cultural expression in an organization). Rapid technology and emerging global economics have sped up the pace of change, while most corporate cultures have not learned to rapidly "transfer" their DNA in order to catch up. In the next decade, there will be a tumultuous period of evolutionary churn. Just like more rapid extinction happens during a major shift in the environment, *many companies will fail during this period of transformation.* Those who survive and thrive will be those who enacted the "genetics of rapid change." This must begin at the very top of the organization. The best HR department in the world can't execute programs to encode and transfer "adaptive DNA" if the top leaders in the company don't believe it is part of their day-to-day job.

Since leaders are the carriers of an organization's DNA, the top leaders' willingness to accept responsibility for growing *more* leaders will ensure an apprentice model of developing leaders has staying power. With or without a formal leadership program, YOU can take responsibility for developing more leaders. YOU can identify promising talent in your company with a desire and aptitude to grow and learn. YOU can be a mentor and share what you have learned. YOU can create an exchange of wisdom and insight about what it means to lead in your company amidst challenging and dynamic conditions.

Providing models of excellence in action is the methodology for good apprenticeship. People learn best by experience, versus being told what to do. At Hindustan Unilever they reflect this in their development model for leaders: 70% of learning takes place on the job, 20% through mentoring, and only 10% in classroom training. There are natural ways to embed learning into your everyday activities. It takes thought and effort to create the systems, but it doesn't require a separate program or investment.

In our collaborative leadership program, we teach the principle of "make your thinking and decision process explicit to people." You need to see your role not just as doing, but as teaching. For example, if you want people to better anticipate problems, start your meeting with a recent story about a problem. Do a short (10 minute) round robin and solicit people's thoughtful ideas about how they would handle the situation. Then, share "what really happened" – for example, how your colleague prevented a major disaster by proactive thinking and problem-solving. This simple structure to your regular staff meetings is a powerful small change in how you mentor your team.

Another example: In reviewing your objectives and strategies (e.g., operations reviews) set them up as a team coaching tool. (Use "well done" and "take a look at" as a feedback roundtable where everyone gets to participate – this is another common tool we use.)

If you want people to act with a greater sense of urgency, ROLE MODEL urgency through shorter, crisper meeting keeping time and writing clear agendas. Make "developing the business" and "growing leaders" simultaneous activities.

Adaptive DNA is passed on through leadership by embedding five SEEDS of change in people and teams:

1. **Self-Awareness.** When leaders are self-aware, they tend to build trust. The foundation of true leadership is strength in oneself first. He is humble and truthful. She welcomes having her ideas and decisions questioned.

2. **External Focus.** A leader whose attention is external can detect change early. She sees an opportunity, a threat, or a weakness before everyone else. He quickly adapts the plan to that reality.

3. **Enable Others.** A true enabler is 100% committed. A committed leader owns his or her power. She enables people and ideas by making passion bigger than fear. He seeks partners in his vision and brings out the best in them, knowing that enabling a vision in business is not a solo act.

4. **Decisive.** The quality of a decisive leader is a bias for action. He always advances the ball forward. She takes calculated risks and is a master of good timing.

5. **Simple is Best.** The quality of simplicity is clarity. Leaders expressing this quality make the complex easily understood. He lives the credo "less is more." She constantly creates shared meaning to catalyze people and resources toward a vision.

Louis (nicknamed Gecko for an uncanny likeness to a certain insurance spokesperson – in voice, not appearance) — describes how he transformed the software group of a major technology company through methods of empowerment and a bias for action. His is a SEEDS of change story – and as you read it, begin to think about how you will start using these principles in your world to enact small changes that benefit you and those around you.

Louis' Story

My favorite leadership credo is: Leaders do the right thing ... managers do things right. Sometimes doing the right thing for the business might mean not following the rules. A manager will sit there and fill in paperwork and pass it to the next person. A leader will look at what's going on and ask: "Why are we filling in this paper every day? Get this person to talk to that person, and skip the paperwork."

For me, that's one of the key tenets of leadership.

When I first came to the U.S. in 2005, I was given a team of 35 people. The condition was terrible: Everybody had to ask for permission and no one had any empowerment. Before any work could begin, the spec had to be written properly and signed off and passed to the design person. The design review had to take place and be properly filed. Then, the API change was requested and that took a month. Then the design work started. Once that was approved, estimates would start, and they would schedule that bit of work with other silos in the organization, who would spend time arguing back and forth about how they were going about it – often for several weeks or months. When schedules were missed, it was always someone else's fault. There was a lot of blaming and no responsibility. People would come in at 9:30 and leave at 3:30. If it didn't quite get done, it didn't get done. They were all veal calves stuck in a barn being fed and doing what they were told. They were the long pole in the tent in this company.

I was replacing the third leader of this group in just under 3 years. I was brought in by an executive who knew this group needed someone who could see things differently. When I arrived, the engineers all believed I was going to lay them all off and move their work to England (where I had come from). They believed it was fait accompli, and they had no say in the matter.

My first move was to get them all in a room to explain the current situation, to let them know what we could achieve, and to paint a vision for the future. I happened to know our company was seeking to outsource our entire software platform; I believed we could change that future, and I wanted them to believe it too.

I explained: Yes, the next project is moving to England. That's because we have to start a new project. And, I need your help to bring that site on board. What you should be more worried about is that the company is likely to outsource our entire software platform to Japan. I want to prove that we can do that work - and get it back in our house. We have to build a coherent platform for the future of this company's products, and I want to own that work, right here. As I spoke, Richard sat in the back with his arms folded looking out the window. The previous manager told me to beware of him — he was a troublemaker, "anti" everything, always giving him a hard time. I know that, often, the biggest cynics become your best change agents. You just have to find out what they're so disgruntled about. With him, I learned he had good ideas but could never put them into action because he was being totally controlled. Today he is one of my key leaders.

So once I laid it out plainly for everyone, a couple of guys up and left. Every other person is still with me 5 years later.

My second move was building a relationship with each person. I sat down one-on-one with each person, and asked a simple series of questions: "What are you working on? How's it going? What problems have you had? What do you see wrong with the organization?" I put a sheet out for each of them so they could write it down. Then, I would ask my favorite line, which I learned from my boss Rob: "I have a magic wand, which is on lease for 30 days before it goes back to Tinkerbell. What can I change for you?" The stuff they told me, I fixed. (Or told them if I really couldn't.) That generated a lot of trust.

My next significant step was to move the measuring stick. Success was redefined as getting the whole process complete, end-to-end. Before, all departments — electronics, op system, UI, work controller — were separate little fiefdoms. I told them "Now, it doesn't matter if someone else is late, you're all accountable to get the whole thing done end-to-end. The job's not done until everything is done. Once you tell me what you can commit to, achieving it is your accountability, not mine. Work with your colleagues across the various departments and get the job done."

And that started the empowerment discussion. I explained that escalating everything (as they had with my predecessor) was not the way to get things done. When someone asks me for a decision, they usually have a preference and just want me to make their decision for them. (Often I deliberately make the one they don't want.) I tell them "Don't ask me what the right thing to do is unless you really don't know. 9 times out of 10 you do know and you're looking for a way to cover your *&%. I shouldn't be making design decisions. You should be sitting down with your partner across the business to make those decisions - to do the right thing. I am constantly reinforcing the message, "Go work with your colleagues and figure it out."

In December (6 months later) Rob asked me to take over a second module. That group was in a completely burned out state. They had three managers overseeing 30 people - and they were dealing with 100 problems per week. They were working 7 days a week, running like crazy but never getting ahead. Everyone was working forced overtime on both Saturdays and Sundays.

The first thing I did was to completely ban forced overtime. I said to my team leads: "If you have to ask people to work overtime, then you don't have true commitment to the project." Through my magic wand process, I found the three thought leaders in the group and said: "You're the team leaders now – you figure out what you need to get the job done. You work it how you want to. And you are accountable to making sure all modules work end-to-end. Now go do the right thing." They said "No one asked us in 3 years, 'What can I do to help?'" They told me what they could achieve, and they met the date THEY committed to. To help them, we turned off testing for 2 weeks so they could get caught up – which totally altered morale. If you let engineers start from zero and get back to zero every week, it is a massive mental motivation for them. People stopped working overtime and figured out how to get the job done in 38 hours a week instead of 60-70 hours per week.

I'm just making those little adjustments all the time. Connecting with people and working with their problems on a daily basis. Each week after my roundtable meeting, I try to take one issue that people want me to change, that I think I can achieve in a week, and get it done.

That's how people gain confidence in you. None of the engineers believed the management team or their leaders were there for them. My style is to let them know I'm there for them. And, I won't overturn something they do. Because if I do, that tells them they are not really accountable. Of course you have to recognize the type of person who can accept that – but that comes from talking to them. You shouldn't give it to someone if they're not ready or wanting it. You have to find the pioneers, not the settlers. You have to keep the bigger picture in sight: "What do we want to build in the organization?" "What kind of culture and behavior do we want?"

Five years later, we've gone from projects taking an average of three years to complete, costing $9 million or more, with a 50% slip rate, to delivering an 11-month, $3 million project with less than 10% slip rate. These two projects had exactly the same scope. And it was not about switching to Agile code; we did this with the same technical barriers we always had. The difference was I focused on building a team that was accountable for an end-to-end result.

If you don't leap out of bed in the morning, look in the mirror excited to get to work, there's something wrong. You can see that happening in these guys now: They are having fun and they like coming to work. One guy got to spend 20% of his time on a "pet project" and used it to create new scan-to-USB code. He told me the next week "I haven't had so much fun in years." Every time someone sends me an email requesting remote access (ie, so they can work from home) I know they are truly committed.

Once you've unleashed people, you don't have to convince them to do anything. The cow is out of the barn; it has seen there is a meadow and a green pasture, and there's no turning back.

Louis planted the SEEDS of small change and cultivated them to create big results. His style is no-nonsense and 100% committed to excellence and results – no excuses allowed! For Louis, the choices to give people free reign and listen carefully are not fluffy feel-good soft platitudes. He simply understands the direct link between a self-directed, motivated workplace culture and the gold pot at the end of the rainbow.

In January of 2010, he was placed in charge of the entire software development function within this organization.

His story is a testimony to what happens when you put aside lofty expectations of "What a leader is supposed to do" – and replace it with a sincere desire to listen, to collaborate, and draw out the best in others. Louis shows us that with the right intention and a few simple questions and tools, anyone can become a leader of small change to create an agile, adaptive, change-friendly culture.

SUMMARY
Nature's Truth #9

In nature, survival is about passing on your DNA.

In business, leaders are the carriers of DNA and need to see a fundamental part of their job as passing it on to the next generation.

Good leadership development helps develop leaders who are not just evaluated by the results they achieve (WHAT), but by HOW they treat people and live the values. (see diagram below). Use these 4 simple steps to build development plans and as the basis for succession planning conversations:

1. Identify your leadership values – which become the values for the team or organization – whatever is your scope of leadership influence. Rate each person on them, on a scale of 1-5

2. Identify desired business results. Rate each person on those, on a scale of 1-5.

3. Plot your team onto the grid. Have them self-assess, and discuss your ratings together.

4. Create individual goals and plans to coach or train the upper left and lower right quadrants

Making it Work! Small Changes for Spreading SEEDS of Leadership DNA

In addition to the practices within SEEDS, our clients are undertaking a simple exercise to create a robust succession and leadership development plan.

Many are not large enterprises where the effort is being led inside HR, but are small- to mid-sized companies or divisions inside larger companies – who want to take charge of apprenticing more leaders, and understand this is how to get out of the trap of "do more with less" and "I have to do it all."

Following is a tool we use to help leaders assess their people on both WHAT they accomplish [Business Results] as well as HOW they accomplish it (Values).

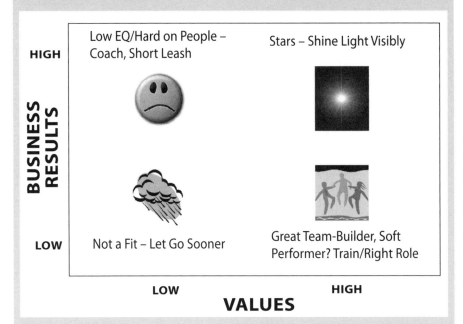

Conclusion

Thank you for joining us for this leadership journey for building a culture that is fit to compete.

Leadership in each organization has one simple goal: Whatever it is you are trying to accomplish, *you go first*. No one is likely to follow if you aren't willing to take the first step. We hope this book will help you take that first step.

If more leaders are like you, able to inspire and enable their people, and view their role as stepping off the beaten paths of old, outdated management methods that keep organizations stuck in place and unable to change, that can be your act of service in these uncertain times.

We are honored to have been a small part of your journey.

May your perfect storm be the catalyst for greater peace and productivity.

Lisa & Gerry
www.CorporateCulturePros.com

Transforming Corporate Culture: Recap

We have covered a lot of territory in this book. Here, we offer three styles of refresher for the major points.

TWITTER SUMMARY

Nature's truths help leaders build a change-friendly corporate culture. It's simpler than you think!

EXECUTIVE SUMMARY

Business change is dizzying!

- Currently we are in the midst of a massive "disruptive transformation" across our global society.

- At work people are increasingly overwhelmed: 2 out of 3 managers and employees are disengaged or actively acting out their dissatisfaction.

- Efforts to implement changes in organizations of every size and scope are failing at an astonishing rate of 75%.

- The "triple-transparency" of globalization, the internet, and outspoken young workers means change is speeding up. Are you keeping the pace?

Corporate culture is the "unseen power source" AND your unique competitive advantage to attract talent. This is how businesses of the future will survive, adapt, and thrive amidst so much complexity. Tapping its power can feel daunting but knowing culture change has a proven process and applying the principle of small change makes it much simpler and easier.

This book draws lessons from the master of change – the natural world – to guide leaders in making small changes and adaptations that mirror how nature performs 3 essential activities:

Create (a solid foundation),

Grow (understand what speeds growth up and what slows it down), and

Evolve (avoid extinction and ensure you're around in 10 years).

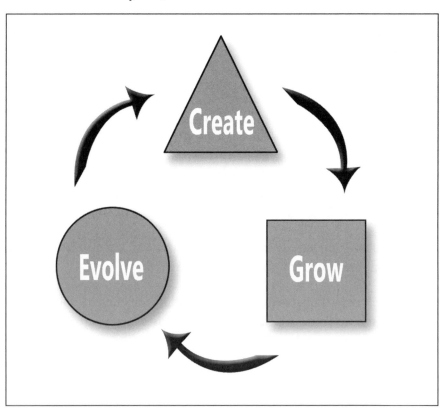

Chapter SUMMARIES

Chapter One: INTENTION
The Seed Is the Tree (or a Dandelion)

Nature's Truth #1:

In nature, everything has a clear purpose to fulfill.

*In business, you must be intentional in reminding
people of the clear purpose behind activity, to avoid
it becoming random or bureaucratic.*

In Chapter 1, we discuss the power of intention. People bring passionate energy to what they are inspired by – and passion is what drives commitment: the foundation of a healthy culture. You can call it engagement, call it involvement, call it empowerment – it's the essential "seed" that creates the tree.

To ensure your change efforts have a strong start, address three important questions:

1. **Are you conscious and transparent about why you are doing what you're doing?**

2. **Does it serve someone besides yourself?**

3. **Will it make the business – or world – better?**

Leaders can cultivate powerful intentions by improving:

1. **Self-awareness – the ability to learn from adversity and tests.**

2. **Commitment – the will to return to your intention and keep going, and surround yourself with people who will help remind you.**

Derek's story of his law firm helps us to illustrate the power of strong intention.

Chapter Two: VISION
Fire Lights the Way

Nature's Truth #2:

In nature, movement typically follows the path of least resistance.

In business, movement forward is catalyzed by shared vision: Vision is the fire of motivation.

In Chapter 2, we explore what makes the concept of vision motivating and real for people, and how you can boost the power of where you are going in a way that people can connect to. This process doesn't need to be based on a grand "save-the-world" vision.

To ensure your Vision is passed like a torch to create a bonfire of shared support, put these small changes in place:

1. **For maximum motivation, use language that helps people commit toward something they want, and away from something they can see should be avoided.**

2. **Build a story to draw out emotion through logic.**

3. **Tell your story often and in many ways: use it as a constant during change.**

Three stories help illustrate this concept: Amtrak's story of transformation; the pharmaceutical executive's vision to "fix the roof or empty the buckets?" and the Starbucks "Fastest Drive-Through Service" challenge.

Chapter 3: TRUST
Is Like the Sun

Nature's Truth #3:

In nature, the sun is the source of all life.

In business, trust is the essential energy in which lasting change can occur, continuously.

In Chapter 3, we explore the role of trust in a healthy culture. The passionate vision leaders carry must build trust, so people believe that the leaders know where we are headed and can take us there.

Leading without trust is a root cause of why change initiatives fail. Imagine trying to feed your family by growing plants in your basement, without grow lights. You are unlikely to produce anything but fungus! Enact these four small change activities, to build strong pillars of trust:

1. Align before you lead; you are hard-wired to connect and be *alike.*

2. Use candor – there is great power in telling the truth with no spin. (For our free tool on "Ten Principles of Candor," visit us on the Web

3. Develop transparency – in today's business climate, people will not trust leaders who hide basic information about the business.

4. Empower people who have earned it.

The insurance company manager's story of how "we've lost our way" and unintentionally built a culture of fear, poignantly illustrates the importance of trust.

Chapter 4: The Structure of GROWTH
Boundaries, Governance, and Guardrails

Nature's Truth #4:

In nature, structure and rules interact perfectly with dynamic, constant change.

In business, structure and governance should be examined to create more collaborative, empowered, and self-accountable workplaces.

In Chapter 4, we explore how effective leaders set up good structures for planning, teamwork and decision making (guardrails and governance) as a framework that change can rest upon.

In the beginning this may seem to slow you down; however, getting everyone aligned about the critical boundaries will speed you up for the long haul: "Go slow to go fast." The following small changes help you provide the right boundaries to enable more rapid growth:

1. **Setting clear goals rarely and creating commitment to them rarely involves the right people** –without overly constraining the business to be nimble and flexible.

2. **A leader's role is to relentlessly narrow and help prioritize during change** – "Where the river narrows, the water moves faster"

3. Use GRPI – or your preferred model to establish clear guardrails during change.

4. Remember emotion is at least as important as logic in making decisions.

5. Clarify Decision Rights in contrast to Nagging Rights.

6. Implement a good decision making process, that answer 3 essential questions: "What is the decision, who is making it, and how will we make it?"

The story of Cathy's goal-setting with clients and Damasio's decision making experiment on the unconscious pull of emotion, help to illustrate how guardrails and governance can support rapid growth.

Chapter 5: COLLABORATE
Power-Up the Tribe!

Nature's Truth #5:

In nature, everything is part of an interactive system.

In business, artificial boundaries must be dissolved to foster more interaction and cooperation.

Chapter 5 explores the tribal model of collaboration, and how to apply this to business. Leaders who do so are masterful at engaging and involving more people sooner – employees, key influencers, suppliers, competitors. Three small change truths will make it easier for you to build a workplace culture of collaborative leadership:

1. We are tribal in nature: We work best when we organize ourselves in a relatively small clan with a shared purpose. Small, empowered teams move faster!

2. The Industrial Age imposed unnatural adversarial relationships between boss and employee, and led to a loss of tribal wisdom in our workplaces. This is the root cause of today's lack of accountability and responsibility. As a leader, see your job as that of asking more questions to foster greater commitment and ownership.

3. We must recreate that wisdom by restoring the best of both worlds into our workplaces – efficiency and productivity along with shared ownership and accountability.

    • Cooperation inside, competition outside

    • Accountability and conflict – help people remember their natural tendency to be personally responsible, and watch how it reduces conflict

The beautiful story of "The Plywood Artwork" teaches us another way of managing conflict.

Chapter 6: COMMUNICATION
Create a Steady Flow

Nature's Truth #6:

In nature, communication flows like water –
endless and non-stop.

In business, information must flow more naturally
and leaders must help build bridges and break down
dams behind which meaning and information are
often stuck.

Chapter 6 explores the importance of communication – which is always flowing regardless of whether it's being directed or managed effectively. We explore clear examples of what people want to know and how to ensure your leadership communication overcomes resistance or apathy to change. Four principles of small change provide clues about getting the flow of communication right:

1. **Commitment is an emotional process, but change is often "sold" as a logical process.**

2. **Communication is always happening. During change, leaders need to manage it to overcome negativity and create positive "pull" toward commitment.**

3. **Frequent, clear communication is how you overcome the natural tendency to resist change. It takes 10-100 times more than you think it will.**

4. **Three laws of motion – inertia, gravity, and resistance – offer clues about the role of leadership communication during change.**

We enjoyed Mark's stories as a navy pilot about communicating in the ultimate change environment: While flying a $50 million aircraft.

Chapter 7: LEARN
Avoid Extinction by Adapting

Nature's Truth #7:

Nature uses learning to avoid extinction.

In business, building a learning culture is the remedy to support an environment of sustainable growth.

In Chapter 7, we discuss learning as nature's way of being adaptable, especially in fast-changing and extreme conditions. We offer ideas for what you can do to create a business culture that reflects learning as its core principle, and embed learning in whatever you do. There are three principles of embedding an effective learning culture:

1. Make sure everyone has a shared understanding of the threats and opportunity for the business. The outcome is to create urgency in everyone.

2. Broaden perspective to detect the need for change, then move faster and adapt more quickly to offset the increasing uncertainty of prediction.

3. Learn to fail and embed a learning mindset in your organization (see practices below)

We heard stories about Rick Arquilla of Roto-Rooter learned from an "up-close view" of his corporate culture as well as Louis' tale of learning and mistakes.

Chapter 8 – MINDSETS
Navigating the Icebergs

Nature's Truth #8:

Nature makes steady, gradual changes to adapt to new conditions.

In business, examining mindsets supports gradual adaptability – they can keep us stuck or help us change when progress is needed.

Chapter 8 explores what is underneath an ability to adapt and change, or not. To grow a great culture means a constant willingness to observe and appreciate the diversity within very small assumptions, ways of being creative, and managing people. How can you manage territorialism and alpha leadership through changing deeper mindsets that drive those behaviors? Use these small change reminders:

1. During change, organizations tend to focus on observable elements: the environment and behavior. Beneath these observable elements are hidden mindsets – the capabilities, mindsets, and identities held by leaders and employees that either reinforce the status quo and allow fear of change to slow progress, or accelerate progress to the desired future.

2. Mindsets have varying strengths – are yours brick, glass, rubber or vapor? Some are harder to change than others.

3. Like "Black Swans," often we ignore the possibility that something might even exist that could transform everything.

4. There are change-derailing and change-friendly mindsets: Learn to notice which are around you and which are *in* you!

The "Black Swan" story reminds us how powerful mindsets can be. After learning a new way of thinking about their parent company, one leadership team secured a $450M investment for their business a year later.

Chapter 9: PROCREATE
Spread Leadership DNA

Nature's Truth #9:

In nature, survival is about passing on your DNA.

In business, leaders are the carriers of DNA and need to see a fundamental part of their job as passing it on.

Chapter 9 is about the role of leaders in spreading their DNA so that there are more people leading, more often, toward a common purpose and goals. How do you repeat and model the behavior you *want*, over and over? Strong, adaptive leaders are not just evaluated by the results they achieve (WHAT), but by HOW they treat people and live the values. Use these 4 simple steps to build development plans and as the basis for succession planning conversations:

1. **Identify your leadership values – which become the values for the team or organization – whatever is your scope of leadership influence. Rate each person on them, on a scale of 1-5**

2. **Identify desired business results. Rate each person on those, on a scale of 1-5.**

3. **Plot your team onto the grid. Have them self-assess, and discuss your ratings together.**

4. **Create individual goals and plans to coach or train the upper left and lower right quadrants**

This chapter included a summary of what the best companies do to develop leaders, based on Fortune magazine's "Best 25 Companies for Leaders." We also heard Louis' story about how he has planted SEEDS of leadership to transform his company's software development group to a high-performing unit that gets the job done on time and on budget.

Transforming Corporate Culture
Discussion Guide:
9 Culture Transforming Questions

The most powerful change occurs through dialogue. Remember sitting on the porch and shooting the breeze? True change happens when you listen to interesting views and perspectives other than your own. Executive teams rarely do enough of this; their meetings and discussions are often too formal and agendas too task-oriented. By asking open-ended questions and spending an hour or two in a lively debate about topics you don't normally discuss, you will evolve your team to foster a valuable insight or idea that you hadn't thought of.

This is the essence of innovation and how an entity grows smarter, faster. And relating in this way is the essence of shaping corporate culture. It begins at the very top.

Here are 9 conversational questions to whet your appetite for powerful, meaningful dialogue. Insert them into the agenda at executive team meetings, and discover how powerful conversations emerge:

1) Is our workplace energized and excited about the future?

2) Why is culture important to us, why now?

3) What is culture to the business: How do we define culture … and how do we define ours?

4) What evidence can we track to let us know the culture of our business is changing with the pace of change in our marketplace?

5) Do our managers and employees believe we have a great workplace culture? How do we know that for sure?

6) Do our VP's and Directors share responsibility for translating our vision so people are ignited by passion and know what's most important for our business right now?

7) Do we as executives have a channel to converse and talk to people on the front lines – to experience the spirit and morale of employees and first-line supervisors and what they need?

8) Are our customers ravings fans of our company? What is the greatest value they perceive from our business?

9) Do we develop our leaders to be great change agents amidst increasing uncertainty and diversity? What could we do to ensure that we are?

What questions come to *your* mind?

Enjoy the challenge of learning from each other ... and above all else, keep the conversation going.

NOTES

Introduction

1. http://en.wikipedia.org/wiki/Employee_engagement - BlessingWhite (April 2008). *2008 Employee Engagement Report*. http://www. blessingwhite.com/eee__report.asp. Retrieved 2008-05-05.

   Gallup website, *Employee Engagement: A Leading Indicator of Financial Performance*, September 7, 2010.

2. Mourier & Smith, 2001, *Conquering Organizational Change*, 2001, citing a review of 26 studies of change efforts.

3. © 2004, Jossey-Bass - A Wiley Imprint

4. © 2008, John Wiley & Sons

5. From *Leadership in a (Permanent) Crisis* by Ronald Heifetz, Alexander Grashow, and Marty Linsky. Copyright © 2009 Harvard Business School Publishing Corporation. All rights reserved.

6. http://www.businessweek.com/magazine/content/09_47/ b4156034717852_page_3.htm
   Is America Falling Off the Flat Earth? 2007, The National Academies Press.

7. http://www.nap.edu/openbook.php?record_id=12021&page=17
   Good Boss, Bad Boss, Robert Sutton, © 2010.

8. The Invincible Apple, Fast Company, July/August 2010.

Chapter 1

9. By William W. George, Peter Sims, Andrew N. McLean, David Mayer, Diana Mayer. Publication date: Feb 01, 2007

Chapter 2

10. From *Leading Change*, John Kotter, Harvard Business Press, May 4, 2009.

11. Excerpted from *The Leadership Solution*, Jim Shaffer, [McGraw-Hill, April 20, 2000]

Chapter 3

12. Erikson, Erik H. *Childhood and Society*. New York: Norton, 1950

13. Reuters News, April 16, 2010.

14. UK : Financial Times / Pearson, 2006.

15. © 2008, *Meeting Minds*

Chapter 4

16. Excerpted from ©Publications International, Ltd. "HowStuffWorks.com" website.2009

17. George Miller, Eugene Galanter and Karl Pribram *"Plans and the Structure of Behavior"* September 1986

18. Excerpted from "When Goals are Dead-Ends," Charles Faulkner, News from the Mental Edge, 1994, www.influentialcommunications.com

19. Excerpted from: Social Intelligence, Daniel Goleman, © 2008

20. *Your Brain at Work: Strategies for Overcoming Distraction, Regaining Focus, and Working Smarter All Day Long,* © 2009, Harper Collins

21. *Neurobiology of Decision-Making* by Antonio Damasio, H. Damasio, Yves Christen; Springer, 1995.

22. Excerpted from *Management Rewired*, Charles S. Jacobs, © 2009, The Penguin Group.

Chapter 5

23. Excerpted from "A Very Short History of Humanity" by George Moromisato
http://neurohack.com/earthguide/History.htm

24. Adapted from; *Management Rewired*, Charles Jacobs, Penguin Books, 2009.

25. Excerpted from and copyrighted by: Saskatchewan Education. (1994). Social Studies: 20 World Issues, Regina, SK.

26. Excerpted from *Indigenous Justice Systems, Tribal Society is a way of life*, by Ada Pecos Melton, published in American Law Journal, December 19, 1995.

27. Source: © 2009 Real People Press. Originally told by Gerry to Mark Andreas, this story will appear in Mark's forthcoming book "Unviolence: true stories of peaceful conflict resolution."

28. http://en.wikipedia.org/wiki/Scrum_(development)

Chapter 7

29. References for complex adaptive systems:

- M. Mitchell Waldrop. (1994). Complexity: the emerging science at the edge of order and chaos. Harmondsworth [Eng.]: Penguin. ISBN 0-14-017968-2.

- K. Dooley, AZ State University

- Complexity in Social Science glossary a research training project of the European Commission

- Peter Fryer. [http://www.trojanmice.com/articles/complexadaptivesystems.htm "A brief description of Complex Adaptive Systems and Complexity Theory"]. http://www.trojanmice.com/articles/complexadaptivesystems.htm. Retrieved 2010-01-24.

Chapter 8

30. Source: http://www.thepracticeofleadership.net/2006/06/25/breaking-your-four-minute-mile/

31. By Kerry Patterson, Joseph Grenny, David Maxfield, Ron McMillan, Al Switzler, McGraw Hill, © 2008

32. Larry Checco © 2008, reprinted with permission. http://nonprofit.about.com/od/nonprofitmanagement/a/herolead.htm

33. Excerpts drawn from "25 Top Companies for Leaders 2009", Fortune magazine, November 19, 2009.

About Corporate Culture Pros

Lisa Jackson

For two decades, Corporate Culture Pros have helped Presidents and their teams lead organizational culture change and align their corporate culture to achieve their business strategy. Our specialty is helping organizations build a culture infrastructure that links directly to hard ROI measures such as market share, profit and innovation.

Gerry Schmidt

The unique and proven culture change process developed by Corporate Culture Pros is effective in turnarounds, mergers, or significant changes in leadership or strategy, when leaders know culture is a competitive advantage.

Questions or comments welcome via: www.CorporateCulturePros.com/contact/ or call 843-588-9286.

Free Corporate Culture Tools

On our website are a series of free tools for changing corporate culture:
http://www.corporateculturepros.com/culture-tools/
We add to these periodically. Sign up via email, Twitter or RSS to receive updates.

Organizational Change Readiness – How likely is it that your innovation or culture change effort will succeed? Pinpoint where trouble spots may trip up your innovation efforts.

Assess Corporate Culture Balance v. Imbalance – Take this assessment to see where your organization's practical daily activities are out of balance and need adjustment.

Changing Corporate Culture Through Tough Conversations – Telling a hard truth is a critical success factor of a corporate culture that can adapt and learn. This tool outlines 10 principles for developing your ability to have tough conversations.

Changing Culture by Improving Decision Making – Most organizations still operate with command-style decision rights; in a global matrix structure this slows down the ability to move at the speed of today's change. This tool outlines a proper decision process in detail.

4 Corporate Culture Types That Hinder Change And Innovation – Is your corporate culture the cause of lack of focus, poor morale, or too much politics? Take a look in the mirror with this tool.

Five Tips for Corporate Cultures of Innovation – Learn the top five tips for building innovation-friendly workplace cultures.

5 Tips to Prepare For Successful Corporate Culture Mergers – According to research, culture is behind the fact that 65-75% of mergers fail to deliver the expected ROI. This tool pinpoints the most important areas to attend to in preparing for a successful merger.